GW00889899

GERMAN

BUSINESSMATE

compiled by
LEXUS
with
Dagmar Förtsch

RICHARD DREW PUBLISHING
Glasgow

RICHARD DREW PUBLISHING LT
6 CLAIRMONT GARDENS
GLASGOW G3 7LW
SCOTLAND

First Published 1983
New Edition 1989
Reprinted 1990

ISBN 0 86267 253 8

Printed in Great Britain by
Cox & Wyman Ltd.

YOUR BUSINESSMATE is specifically designed to be of maximum service to you on your business trip to Germany, Austria, Switzerland or East Germany (or if you are having German-speaking visitors here in Britain). The BUSINESSMATE gives you one single A–Z list of terms and expressions to help you communicate efficiently in German:

* at the sales meeting
* in discussing terms, contracts, schedules
* in looking at figures and accounts
* in finding solutions and making plans

And in addition to this you'll find words and phrases that will be useful when you are

* travelling
* at your hotel
* coping with typical business trip problems

Built into the A–Z list, for speed and ease of reference, there are some 400 German words, German abbreviations and acronyms that you'll find on documents, statements, on balance sheets, invoices, notices etc. There is factual and practical information too: travel tips (see accommodation, train etc); conversion tables (see foot, pint etc); a menu reader (see menu); a wine guide (see wine); a schnaps guide (see schnaps); numbers are on pages 188–189 and there is a map on page 6.

On pages 4 to 5 there are notes on the pronunciation of German.

All in all, your BUSINESSMATE will make for a smoother, more efficient trip. If you are in business then

this book means business

Pronouncing German

Compared with English, German is a very regular pronouncing language, that is to say: there is a far more consistent relationship between a letter or group of letters and the sounds that these letters will have. General guidelines to pronunciation are as follows: One key rule to remember is that German pronounces every syllable of a word. So for example, 'Analyse' in German is spoken [an-a-loo-zuh].

a   as in *father*: Tag, bat, ratsam, fahren, schwarz
     as in *mat*: hatte, Kampagne, gesamt, hat, ab
e   as in *play*: zehn, geben, Kredit
     as in *bed*: Rechnung, Geld, wetten
     as in *hair*: Verbraucher, per, werden, fern
     as in *father*: ge-, Kunde, gehen, Käufer
i   as in *seen*: wir, ihr
     as in *sit*: in, ist, -isch, bitte
o   as in *tone*: so, Lohn, Boot, Brot
     as in *hot*: kommen, Soll, ob
     as in *sort*: Sorte, Wort, vor
u   as in *soon*: zu, tun, Buch, Einfuhr
     as in *book*: um, un-, -ung, Schluß
ä   as in *play*: spät, später
     as in *bed*: hätte, Änderung
ö   as in *her*: können, möchte
ü,y as in *huge* without the 'j' sound: über, Gebühr, analysieren
au as in *how*, *cow*
äu as in *boy*, *toy*
ee as in *hay*, *day*
ei as in *ice*, *pie*
eu as in *boy*, *toy*
ie as in *team*, *seen*

Consonants are as in English with the following main differences:
b   in final position becomes p: ab [ap]

ch after a, au, o, u as in the Scottish
    pronunciation of loch; after other sounds
    similar to sh
d   in final position becomes t: Hand [hant]
g   as in good
j   as in yacht
qu =kv
s   in initial position becomes z: Soll [zoll];
    Phase [fah-zuh]
ß   =ss
sch =sh
sp/st in initial position become shp/sht: spät
    [shpayt]; Stand [shtannt]
th =t
v   =f
w   =v
z   =ts

The German alphabet
a [ah] b [bay] c [tsay] d [day] e [ay] f [eff] g [gay]
h [hah] i [ee] j [yot] k [kah] l [el] m [em] n [en]
o [oh] p [pay] q [koo] r [air] s [ess] t [tay] u [oo]
v [fow] w [vay] x [iks] y [oop-see-lon] z [tset]

Genders
German has three genders: masculine, feminine
and neuter. The word for 'the' can therefore be
either 'der', 'die' or 'das'; and the corresponding
forms of 'a' are 'ein', 'eine', 'ein'. In this book we
have given whichever article seems more likely
given an actual context of usage. For example:
'ein Whisky' but 'die Rechnung'.

Feminine forms of nouns are made by adding
--in. For example: Engländer (Englishman)/
Engländerin (Englishwoman).

a, an ein/eine/ein
   10 marks a litre zehn Mark der Liter
Abf.=Abfahrt departures
Abfindung settlement
Abgabe tax
Abkommen agreement
abkömmlich available
Abnahme purchase; drop
Abnahmemenge amount purchased
Abnehmer purchaser; customer
about: is he about? ist er da?
   about 15 ungefähr fünfzehn
   at about 2 o'clock gegen zwei Uhr
above über
   above that darüber
above-mentioned oben genannt
Abrechnung settlement; statement; account
abroad im Ausland
   to go abroad ins Ausland fahren
Abruf call (on goods)
Abs.=Absender sender
Absatz sales
Abschluß conclusion (of contract, deal)
Abschreibungen depreciation
Abt.=Abteilung department
abzgl.=abzüglich minus, less
accept annehmen
   we accept your proposal wir nehmen Ihren
   Vorschlag an
acceptable annehmbar
acceptance die Annahme

ä [eh], au as in h*ow*, äu, eu [oy], ei as in I, ie [ee]
ö as in h*er*, ü, y as in h*uge*, -b [-p], -d [-t], j [y], qu [kv]
s- [z-], ß [ss], v [f], w [v], z [ts]

acceptance trials die Abnahmeprüfung
accommodation die Unterkunft
   we need accommodation for three wir
   brauchen Zimmer für drei
   » *TRAVEL TIP: as well as hotels there is the 'Hotel*
   Garni' (bed and breakfast), 'Pension' (boarding
   house), 'Gasthof' (inn) or a room in a private
   house; look for the sign 'Zimmer frei' or
   'Fremdenzimmer'; information on local
   accommodation from railway station, look for
   'Zimmernachweis' or tourist information office
accordance: in accordance with your wishes
   Ihren Wünschen entsprechend
according: according to Herr Braun laut
   Herrn Braun
   according to the contract nach dem Vertrag
account (*bank*) das Konto
   (*bill*) die Rechnung
   (*customer*) der Kunde
   15% on account fünfzehn Prozent als
   Anzahlung
   that will be taken into account das werden
   wir berücksichtigen
account number die Kontonummer
accountant der Wirtschaftsprüfer
   (*in company*) der Buchhalter
   (*for tax purposes*) der Steuerberater
accounting method das Buchungsverfahren
accounting period der Buchungszeitraum
accounts: our accounts for the past year
   unsere Abrechnung für das Vorjahr
   may we look at your accounts for 1983?
   können wir Ihren Jahresabschluß für 1983
   sehen?
accounts department die Buchhaltung
accurate genau
Achtung *caution, danger; (spoken) look out!;*
   (announcement) attention please
acknowledge bestätigen

across über
across-the-board allgemein
action: what action are you going to take?
  welche Maßnahmen werden Sie ergreifen?
actual (*as against targeted*) tatsächlich
actuary der Aktuar
ADAC=Allgemeiner Deutscher Automobil-
  Club equivalent of AA or RAC
adaptor der Adapter
additional zusätzlich
address die Adresse
  will you give me your address? können Sie
  mir bitte Ihre Adresse geben?
adequate ausreichend
  that's quite adequate das ist ganz
  angemessen
administration die Verwaltung
admission (*of truth etc*) das Eingeständnis
adults Erwachsene
advance: in advance im voraus
  can we book in advance? können wir im
  voraus buchen?
  advance payment die Vorauszahlung
advantage der Vorteil
advertisement die Annonce
  (*for product*) die Anzeige
  I want to put an advertisement in the
  paper ich möchte in der Zeitung inserieren
advertising die Werbung
advertising campaign die Werbekampagne
advice: we would appreciate advice as to
  when ... würden Sie uns bitte Bescheid geben,
  wann ...
advice note die Benachrichtigung
advisable ratsam

ä [eh], au as in h*ow*, äu, eu [oy], ei as in I, ie [ee]
ö as in h*er*, ü, y as in h*u*ge, -b [-p], -d [-t], j [y], qu [kv]
s- [z-], ß [ss], v [f], w [v], z [ts]

....

advise: please advise us bitte teilen Sie uns mit
  we have been advised that ... es wurde uns mitgeteilt, daß ...
afraid: I'm afraid I don't know das weiß ich leider nicht
  I'm afraid so ja, leider
  I'm afraid not leider nicht
after: after you nach Ihnen
  after 2 o'clock nach zwei Uhr
afternoon der Nachmittag
  in the afternoon nachmittags
  this afternoon heute nachmittag
  good afternoon guten Tag!
after sales service der Service
AG [ah-gay] = *Aktiengesellschaft public share company; reserves a minimum of 5 founding directors; reserves of at least 10% of share capital must be maintained for liability requirements*
again wieder
against gegen
  against the dollar gegenüber dem Dollar
age das Alter
  it takes ages das dauert eine Ewigkeit
agency die Vertretung
agency agreement das Vertretungsabkommen *see* **sole**
agenda die Tagesordnung
  on the agenda auf der Tagesordnung
agent der Vertreter
AGM die Jahreshauptversammlung
ago: a week ago vor einer Woche
  it wasn't long ago das ist noch nicht lange her
  how long ago was that? wie lange ist das her?
agree: I agree ich bin ganz Ihrer Meinung
  I can't agree with that dem kann ich nicht zustimmen

if we can agree on a solution wenn wir uns
auf eine Lösung einigen können
do you agree that this is too much?
stimmen Sie zu, daß das zu viel ist?
agreeable: if you are agreeable wenn Sie
zustimmen
agreement die Vereinbarung
we're in agreement on that darin sind wir
uns einig
let's try to reach an agreement wir wollen
doch versuchen, zu einer Übereinkunft zu
kommen
you broke the agreement Sie haben sich
nicht an die Abmachung gehalten
aim (*of talks etc*) das Ziel
air die Luft
by air per Flugzeug
by airmail per Luftpost
airfreight die Luftfracht
we'll airfreight them to you wir werden sie
Ihnen per Luftfracht zustellen
airport der Flughafen
air waybill der Luftfrachtbrief
Akkreditiv letter of credit
Aktenzeichen file reference
Aktie share
Aktiva assets
alarm der Alarm
alarm clock der Wecker
alcohol der Alkohol
all: all the people alle Leute
all night/all day die ganze Nacht/den ganzen
Tag
that's all wrong das ist ganz falsch
all right? in Ordnung?

ä [eh], au as in h*ow*, äu, eu [oy], ei as in I, ie [ee]
ö as in h*er*, ü, y as in h*u*ge, -b [-p], -d [-t], j [y], qu [kv]
s- [z-], ß [ss], v [f], w [v], z [ts]

that's all das ist alles
thank you — not at all danke — bitte, gern
geschehen
allow erlauben
will you allow us more time? können Sie uns
mehr Zeit geben?
allowance (*discount etc*) der Rabatt
promotion allowance die Werbegelder
allowed erlaubt
is it allowed? ist es erlaubt?
it's not allowed das ist verboten!
allow me gestatten Sie
almost fast
alone allein
already schon
also auch
alter ändern
alteration die Änderung
when we've carried out the alterations
wenn wir die Änderungen vorgenommen
haben
although obwohl
altogether insgesamt
always immer
a.m. vormittags
ambassador der Botschafter
ambulance der Krankenwagen
» *TRAVEL TIP: dial 110*
amendment (*to contract etc*) die Änderung
America Amerika
American amerikanisch
(*person*) Amerikaner/Amerikanerin
among unter
amount der Betrag
the total amount der Gesamtbetrag
it amounts to more than ... es kommt auf
über ...
an *on*
analyse analysieren

analysis die Analyse
and und
Angebot offer
angry verärgert
  I'm very angry about it ich bin darüber sehr
  verärgert
  please don't get angry bitte ärgern Sie sich
  nicht
Anhang appendix
Ankft.=Ankunft arrivals
Anlage enclosure (in letter)
Anlieger frei residents only
Anmeldung reception
annoy ärgern
  it's very annoying das ist sehr ärgerlich
annual jährlich, Jahres-
annual accounts die Jahresabrechnung
annual report der Jahresbericht
another: can we have another room? können
  wir ein anderes Zimmer haben?
  another beer, please noch ein Bier, bitte
answer die Antwort
  what was his answer? was hat er darauf
  gesagt?
  there was no answer es hat sich niemand
  gemeldet
Antrag application
Antwort reply
Anwalt lawyer
any irgendein
  have you got any suggestions? haben Sie
  Vorschläge?
  I haven't got any ich habe keine
anybody (irgend) jemand
anyhow jedenfalls

ä [eh], au as in h*ow*, äu, eu [oy], ei as in I, ie [ee]
ö as in h*er*, ü, y as in h*u*ge, -b [-p], -d [-t], j [y], qu [kv]
s- [z-], ß [ss], v [f], w [v], z [ts]

anything (irgend) etwas
  I don't want anything ich möchte gar nichts
aperitif ein Aperitif
apology eine Entschuldigung
  please accept our apologies wir bitten um
  Entschuldigung
  I want an apology ich warte auf eine
  Entschuldigung
appendix (*to contract*) der Anhang
application form das Antragsformular
  (*for job*) das Bewerbungsformular
apply: to apply for a grant einen Zuschuß
  beantragen
  to apply for a job sich um eine Stelle
  bewerben
  that doesn't apply in this case das trifft in
  diesem Fall nicht zu
appointment ein Termin
  can I make an appointment? kann ich einen
  Termin vereinbaren?
  I've an appointment ich habe einen Termin
appreciate: we appreciate your problem wir
  verstehen Ihr Problem
  yes, I appreciate that, but ... ja, ich sehe das
  ein, aber ...
  we would appreciate it if you could ... wir
  wären Ihnen dankbar, wenn Sie ... könnten
  thank you, I appreciate it vielen Dank, sehr
  nett von Ihnen
  it actually appreciates in value es steigt
  tatsächlich im Wert
appreciation: as a sign of our appreciation
  als Zeichen unserer Anerkennung
approach: our approach to distribution
  unsere Art des Vertriebs
  you should approach our agents Sie sollten
  sich an unsere Vertreter wenden
  we have been approached by another firm
  eine andere Firma ist an uns herangetreten

have they been making approaches to you? haben Sie versucht, an Sie heranzutreten?

appropriate: the appropriate department die zuständige Abteilung

at the appropriate time zur rechten Zeit

approval die Zustimmung

not without your approval nicht ohne Ihre Zustimmung

approve: do you approve? halten Sie es für gut?

you have to approve these changes Sie müssen diese Änderungen genehmigen

approximately etwa, zirka

April April

Arbeit work; job

area die Gegend

area manager der Regionalbeauftragte

arm der Arm

around um ... herum

arrange: will you arrange it? können Sie das arrangieren?

it's all arranged es ist alles arrangiert

that's easily arranged das läßt sich leicht machen

arrangement: we have a special arrangement with them wir haben ein besonderes Abkommen mit ihnen

can we discuss the arrangements? können wir über die Pläne diskutieren?

all the arrangements have been made alle Vorkehrungen sind getroffen

arrears Rückstände

you have arrears of ... Sie sind mit ... im Rückstand

ä [eh], au as in how, äu, eu [oy], ei as in I, ie [ee]
ö as in her, ü, y as in huge, -b [-p], -d [-t], j [y], qu [kv]
s- [z-], ß [ss], v [f], w [v], z [ts]

....

payments are in arrears die Zahlungen sind
im Rückstand
arrival die Ankunft
arrive ankommen
  we only arrived yesterday wir sind erst
  gestern angekommen
art die Kunst
artificial künstlich
as: as quickly as you can so schnell Sie können
  as much as you can so viel Sie können
  as you like wie Sie wünschen
  as of today ab heute
  see **per**
a.s.a.p. so bald wie möglich
ashtray ein Aschenbecher
ask fragen
  could you ask him to ...? könnten Sie ihn
  bitten, ... zu ...?
  that's not what I asked for das habe ich
  nicht bestellt
  I have been asked to tell you ... man hat
  mich gebeten, Ihnen mitzuteilen, daß ...
asleep: he's still asleep er schläft noch
aspirin eine Kopfschmerztablette
assembly (*of machine*) die Montage
assembly instructions die Montageanleitung
assets das Vermögen
  (*on balance sheet*) Aktiva
assistant der Assistent
assistant manager der stellvertretende
  Geschäftsführer
assume: I assume ... ich nehme an, ...
  can we safely assume that ...? können wir
  mit Sicherheit davon ausgehen, daß ...?
assumption die Annahme
  that's just an assumption das ist nur eine
  Vermutung
assurance: you have my assurance that ... ich
  versichere Ihnen, daß ...

assure: could you assure us that ...? könnten
  Sie uns versichern, daß ...?
  rest assured Sie können sich darauf verlassen
at: at the airport am Flughafen
  at my hotel in meinem Hotel
  at one o'clock um ein Uhr
  at 15% zu fünfzehn Prozent
  at his request auf seine Bitte hin
atmosphere die Atmosphäre
attach beifügen
  the attached invoice die beiliegende
  Rechnung
attaché case der Aktenkoffer
attention: for the attention of Mr ... zu Händen
  Herrn ..., z.Hd. Herrn ...
  please pay special attention to ... bitte
  achten Sie besonders auf ...
  thank you for bringing it to our attention
  wir danken Ihnen, daß Sie uns darauf
  aufmerksam gemacht haben
attitude die Einstellung
attractive attraktiv
audit: after last year's audit nach der
  Buchprüfung des Vorjahres
auditor der Buchprüfer
Auftrag order
Aufzug lift
August August
aus off
Ausfahrt exit
Ausfuhr export
Ausführung: in zweifacher/dreifacher
  Ausführung in duplicate/triplicate
Ausgang exit
Auskunft information

ä [eh], au as in h*ow*, äu, eu [oy], ei as in I, ie [ee]
ö as in h*er*, ü, y as in h*u*ge, -b [-p], -d [-t], j [y], qu [kv]
s- [z-], ß [ss], v [f], w [v], z [ts]

....

außer Betrieb *out of order*
Australia Australien
Australian australisch
Austria Österreich
Austrian österreichisch
  (*person*) Österreicher/Österreicherin
Ausverkauf sale
ausverkauft *sold out*
authority: I need my director's authority ich
  brauche die Zustimmung meines Chefs
  do we have your authority to ...? haben wir
  Ihre Vollmacht ... zu ...?
authorities die Behörden
authorize (*steps, decision*) genehmigen
  I'm not authorized to ... ich bin nicht
  berechtigt, ...
automatic automatisch
  (*car*) der Automatikwagen
automatically automatisch
autumn der Herbst
  in the autumn im Herbst
availability: subject to availability
  Lieferbarkeit vorbehalten
available (*goods*) lieferbar
  (*person*) frei
  on the next available flight mit dem
  nächstmöglichen Flug
average der Durchschnitt
  only average results nur durchschnittliche
  Ergebnisse
  above/below average über/unter dem
  Durchschnitt
avoid: to avoid delay um eine Verzögerung zu
  vermeiden
await: we are awaiting ... wir warten auf ...
  awaiting your prompt reply wir sehen Ihrer
  umgehenden Antwort mit Interesse entgegen
aware: are you aware of the ...? sind Sie sich
  über ... im klaren?

away weg
  is it far away from here? ist es weit weg von hier?
awful schrecklich
Az.=Aktenzeichen file reference
back: **I'll be right back** ich bin gleich wieder da
  is he back? ist er zurück?
  when will he be back? wann ist er wieder da?
  can I have my money back? kann ich mein Geld wiederhaben?
  come back kommen Sie zurück!
  I go back tomorrow ich fahre morgen zurück
  at the back hinten
  we'll get back to you on that wir werden in dieser Angelegenheit noch auf Sie zurückkommen
backer *(for scheme)* der Geldgeber
backing die Unterstützung
  we need your backing wir brauchen Ihre Unterstützung
backlog *(of work)* die Arbeitsrückstände
  (of orders) die Auftragsrückstände
back out: **I'm afraid you can't back out** Sie können leider nicht mehr davon zurücktreten
  they backed out at the last minute sie haben sich in letzter Minute noch zurückgezogen
back up: **the figures back it up** die Zahlen bestätigen das
back-up die Unterstützung
Bad bathroom
bad schlecht
  too bad Pech!
  bad debts zweifelhafte Forderungen
baggage das Gepäck
Bahnsteig platform

ä [eh], au as in h*o*w, äu, eu [oy], ei as in I, ie [ee]
ö as in h*er*, ü, y as in h*u*ge, -b [-p], -d [-t], j [y], qu [kv]
s- [z-], ß [ss], v [f], w [v], z [ts]

....

balance die Bilanz
   (*on bank statement, accounts*) der Saldo
   (*remainder*) der Rest
  on balance alles in allem
balance out: they balance each other out sie
  gleichen sich aus
balance sheet die Bilanz(aufstellung)
ball-point pen der Kugelschreiber
bank die Bank
bank account das Bankkonto
bank draft der Wechsel
bank loan das Darlehen
bank manager der Bankdirektor
  my bank manager der Leiter meiner
  Bankfiliale
bankrupt bankrott
bar die Bar
barber's der (Herren)friseur
bargain: it's a real bargain das ist wirklich
  günstig
base (*HQ*) die Zentrale
  our German base unsere deutsche
  Niederlassung
  it's based on the assumption that ... es geht
  von der Annahme aus, daß ...
basic (*problem, product, interest*) grundlegend
basically im Grunde genommen
basis die Grundlage
  as a basis for negotiations als
  Verhandlungsgrundlage
bath das Bad
bathroom das Badezimmer
  I'd like a room with a private bathroom ich
  hätte gern ein Zimmer mit Bad
battery die Batterie
be: to be sein
  don't be ... seien Sie nicht ...
  be reasonable seien Sie vernünftig
  see **he, you, they** *etc*

Beamte(r) *official; civil servant*
beat: to beat the competition die Konkurrenz
  schlagen
  we can beat these prices wir können diese
  Preise unterbieten
beautiful schön
  that was a beautiful meal das Essen war
  ausgezeichnet
because weil
  because of the delay wegen der Verzögerung
bed das Bett
  single bed/double bed ein Einzelbett/
  Doppelbett
  I'm off to bed ich geh' ins Bett
  bed and breakfast Übernachtung mit
  Frühstück
Bedarf *demand*
Bedingung *condition*
bedroom das Schlafzimmer
beer ein Bier
  two beers, please zwei Bier, bitte
  YOU MAY THEN HEAR …
  Pils oder Export? *pils or export? (pils is
  stronger)*
  große oder kleine? *large or small?*
  (large=0.5 litre, small=0.2)
  eine Halbe=½*litre=0.9 pints*
  eine Maß *typical in Bavaria=1 litre; if you like
  a darker beer try 'ein Alt', though this is not
  available in all parts of Germany*
befördern *to transport*
before: before breakfast vor dem Frühstück
  before we leave bevor wir gehen
  I haven't been here before ich war noch nie
  hier

ä [eh], au as in h*o*w, äu, eu [oy], ei as in I, ie [ee]
ö as in h*er*, ü, y as in h*u*ge, -b [-p], -d [-t], j [y], qu [kv]
s- [z-], ß [ss], v [f], w [v], z [ts]

....

begin anfangen
  when does it begin? wann fängt es an?
  beginning next month ab nächsten Monat
behalf: on behalf of Mr Stevens im Auftrag
  von Herrn Stevens
  (*as spokesman for*) im Namen von Herrn
  Stevens
  on your/his behalf in Ihrem/seinem Auftrag
behind hinter
  we're behind on delivery wir sind mit der
  Lieferung in Verzug geraten
Belgian belgisch
Belgium Belgien
believe: I don't believe you das glaub' ich
  (Ihnen) nicht
  I believe you das glaub' ich Ihnen
bell die Klingel
belong: that belongs to me das gehört mir
  who does this belong to? wem gehört das?
below unter
beneficiary (*of letter of credit*) der Begünstigte
Bericht report
berth (*on ship*) das Bett
Beruf profession
Bescheinigung certificate
Beschwerde complaint
besetzt engaged; (*bus*) full
beside neben
Besprechung discussion
best beste(r,s)
  we'll do our best wir werden unser
  möglichstes tun
Bestätigung confirmation
Bestellnummer order number
Bestellung order
Betr. Re
Betrag amount
Betreten verboten no trespassing
better besser

haven't you got anything better? haben Sie nichts Besseres?
are you feeling better? geht es Ihnen besser?
I'm feeling a lot better es geht mir viel besser
between zwischen
Bevollmächtigung authorization
bewachter Parkplatz supervised car park
beyond über
Bezahlung payment
Bezug reference
bid das Angebot
big groß
  a big one ein großer, eine große, ein großes
  that's too big das ist zu groß
  it's not big enough das ist nicht groß genug
  have you got a bigger one? haben Sie nichts Größeres?
bill die Rechnung
  could I have the bill, please? bitte zahlen
bill of exchange der Wechsel
bill of lading der Frachtbrief
bit: just a bit nur ein bißchen
  that's a bit too expensive das ist ein bißchen zu teuer
  just a little bit for me nur ganz wenig für mich
  a big bit ein großes Stück
bitte eintreten please enter
bitte klingeln please ring
bitte klopfen please knock
bitte nicht stören please do not disturb
black schwarz
  in the black im Plus
blood pressure: I've got high blood pressure ich habe hohen Blutdruck

---

ä [eh], au as in h*o*w, äu, eu [oy], ei as in I, ie [ee]
ö as in h*e*r, ü, y as in h*u*ge, -b [-p], -d [-t], j [y], qu [kv]
s- [z-], ß [ss], v [f], w [v], z [ts]

blue blau

BLZ=Bankleitzahl *bank code*

board (*of directors*) der Aufsichtsrat

  board meeting die Vorstandssitzung

  full board Vollpension

  half board Halbpension

  boarding pass die Bordkarte

boat das Boot

  (*bigger*) das Schiff

boat train die Zugfähre

bona fide echt

bonded warehouse das Zolldepot

bonus die Prämie [pray-mee-uh]

book das Buch

  your books Ihre Bücher

  can I book a seat for ...? kann ich einen Platz für ... bestellen?

  I'd like to book a seat for ... ich möchte einen Platz für ... bestellen

  I'd like to book a table for two ich möchte einen Tisch für zwei Personen bestellen

  YOU MAY THEN HEAR ...

  wie war der Name, bitte? *what name please?*

  für wann, bitte? *for what time?*

booking office die Kasse

bookshop die Buchhandlung

border die Grenze

boring langweilig

born: I was born in ... ich bin in ... geboren

  see **date**

borrow borgen

borrowings die Anleihen

Börse *Stock Exchange*

boss der Chef

both beide

  I'll take both of them ich nehme beide

bottle die Flasche

bottom: at the bottom of the list unten auf der Liste

box die Schachtel
  (*wood*) die Kiste
boy ein Junge
brake die Bremse
  I had to brake suddenly ich mußte plötzlich
  bremsen
  he didn't brake er hat nicht gebremst
branch die Zweigstelle, die Filiale
branch manager der Zweigstellenleiter, der
  Filialleiter
branch office die Zweigstelle, die Filiale
brand die Marke
brand awareness das Markenbewußtsein
brand image das Markenimage
brandy der Kognak
breach: they are in breach of contract sie
  sind vertragsbrüchig geworden
bread das Brot
  could we have some bread and butter?
  können wir etwas Brot und Butter haben?
  some more bread, please noch etwas Brot,
  bitte
break (*contract, agreement*) brechen
  it was you who broke the contract Sie sind
  vertragsbrüchig geworden
breakdown (*of figures*) die Aufschlüsselung
  could you give me a complete breakdown?
  können Sie mir eine vollständige
  Aufschlüsselung geben?
  (*of car, machine*) die Panne
» *TRAVEL TIP: motorway patrols give free help*
  (except parts); telephone for 'Straßenwachthilfe'
break even plus-minus-null abschließen
  at that rate we don't even break even so
  decken wir nicht einmal unsere Kosten

ä [eh], au as in h*ow*, äu, eu [oy], ei as in I, ie [ee]
ö as in h*er*, ü, y as in h*u*ge, -b [-p], -d [-t], j [y], qu [kv]
s- [z-], ß [ss], v [f], w [v], z [ts]

breakeven point der Break-even-point, die
  Gewinnschwelle
breakfast das Frühstück
  English/Continental breakfast englisches/
  kleines Frühstück
briefcase die Aktentasche
**briefing: please give me a full briefing on the
  situation** geben Sie mir bitte genaue
  Informationen zur Sachlage
brilliant großartig
bring bringen
  could you bring it to my hotel? können Sie
  es mir bitte ins Hotel bringen?
**bring forward: we've brought the date
  forward three weeks** wir haben den Termin
  um drei Wochen vorverlegt
Britain Großbritannien
British britisch
  the British die Briten
  I'm British ich bin Brite
  (*woman*) ich bin Britin
brochure der Prospekt
  have you got any brochures about ...?
  haben Sie Prospekte über ...?
broken kaputt
  you've broken it Sie haben es kaputt
  gemacht
  my room/car has been broken into man ist
  in mein Zimmer/meinen Wagen eingebrochen
broker der Makler
brought forward übertragen
  amount brought forward der Übertrag
brown braun
browse: can I just browse around? kann ich
  mich mal umsehen?
brutto *gross*
budget der Etat [ay-tah], das Budget [boodjay]
budgeting die Kalkulation
buffet das Büffet

....

build bauen
building das Gebäude
bunch of flowers ein Blumenstrauß
Bundesrepublik Deutschland *Federal*
   Republic of Germany
bunk das Bett
   (*in ship*) die Koje
buoyant (*market*) rege
Büro *office*
bus der Bus
   bus stop die Bushaltestelle
   could you tell me when we get there?
   können Sie mir bitte sagen, wo ich aussteigen
   muß?
» *TRAVEL TIP: bus travel; on town bus routes you*
   may have to buy your ticket from a machine
   near the bus stop before you get on the bus
business das Geschäft
   I'm here on business ich bin geschäftlich hier
   business trip die Geschäftsreise
   we have a business proposition to put to
   you wir möchten Ihnen ein Geschäft
   vorschlagen
   we look forward to doing more business
   with you wir würden uns über weitere
   geschäftliche Zusammenarbeit mit Ihnen
   freuen
   it's a pleasure to do business with you die
   Zusammenarbeit mit Ihnen ist uns ein
   Vergnügen
   our business relationship unsere
   Geschäftsverbindung
   that's not our way of doing business mit
   solchen Methoden arbeiten wir nicht
   business is business Geschäft ist Geschäft

ä [eh], au as in h*o*w, äu, eu [oy], ei as in I, ie [ee]
ö as in h*er*, ü, y as in h*u*ge, -b [-p], -d [-t], j [y], qu [kv]
   s- [z-], ß [ss], v [f], w [v], z [ts]

busy beschäftigt
   (*telephone*) besetzt
   are you busy? haben Sie viel zu tun?
   we're very busy these days wir haben in
   letzter Zeit viel zu tun
but aber
   not ... but ... nicht ..., sondern ...
butter die Butter
button der Knopf
buy kaufen
   where can I buy ...? wo kann ich ... kaufen?
   I'll buy it ich nehme es
   nobody's buying them keiner kauft sie
   our company has been bought by ... unsere
   Firma wurde von ... aufgekauft
   we'll buy up the remaining stock wir
   kaufen die restlichen Bestände auf
buyer der (Ein)käufer
buying department der Einkauf
by: I'm here by myself ich bin allein hier
   can you do it by January? können Sie das
   bis Januar erledigen?
   by train/car/plane per Bahn/Auto/Flugzeug
   by the station am Bahnhof
   who's it made by? wer ist der Hersteller?
   signed by ... von ... unterschrieben
bzw.=beziehungsweise or; respectively
ca.=circa about, approx
cabin (*on ship*) die Kabine
cable (*message*) ein Telegramm
cafe ein Café
» *TRAVEL TIP: in the 'Konditorei' or 'Café' you*
   will get mostly coffee and cakes; alcohol and
   snacks are served too; for a fuller café-type meal
   go to an 'Imbißstube' or 'Schnellimbiß';
   otherwise a pub
cake der Kuchen
   a piece of cake ein Stück Kuchen
calculate kalkulieren

calculator der Rechner
call (*on goods*) der Abruf
call: will you call the manager? rufen Sie bitte
den Geschäftsführer!
    what is this called? wie heißt das?
    he'll be calling on you next week er wird
nächste Woche bei Ihnen vorbeikommen
    I'll call you back ich rufe zurück
    see **telephone**
call box die Telefonzelle
calm ruhig
    calm down beruhigen Sie sich
camera die Kamera
campaign eine Kampagne
can: can you ...? können Sie ...?
    I can't ... ich kann nicht ...
    he can't ... er kann nicht ...
    we can't ... wir können nicht ...
    can they ...? können sie ...?
Canada Kanada
Canadian kanadisch
cancel (*order*) stornieren
    I want to cancel my booking ich möchte
meine Buchung rückgängig machen
    can we cancel dinner for tonight? können
wir das Abendessen für heute abbestellen?
    the flight has been cancelled der Flug fällt
aus
cancellation die Stornierung
capacity die Kapazität
capital (*money*) das Kapital
capital assets Kapitalanlagen
capital equipment Anlagegüter
capital expenditure der Kapitalaufwand
capital-intensive kapitalintensiv

ä [eh], au as in h*ow*, äu, eu [oy], ei as in I, ie [ee]
ö as in h*er*, ü, y as in h*u*ge, -b [-p], -d [-t], j [y], qu [kv]
s- [z-], ß [ss], v [f], w [v], z [ts]

car das Auto
carafe eine Karaffe
card: business card die Geschäftskarte
   do you have a card? haben Sie eine
   Geschäftskarte?
**care: will you take care of my briefcase for
   me?** würden Sie bitte auf meine Aktentasche
   aufpassen?
careful: be careful seien Sie vorsichtig
car-ferry die Autofähre
cargo die Fracht
car park der Parkplatz
   (*indoors*) das Parkhaus
carriage paid frei Haus
carrier der Spediteur
carry: will you carry this for me? können Sie
   das bitte für mich tragen?
carry forward übertragen
carry on weitermachen
   please carry on as before machen Sie bitte
   so weiter wie bisher
carry out: not properly carried out nicht
   richtig durchgeführt
   we've carried out your request wir haben
   Ihren Wünschen Folge geleistet
carton der Karton
case (*suitcase*) der Koffer
   (*packing case*) die Kiste
   in that case in diesem Fall
   or as the case may be je nachdem
   in such cases in solchen Fällen
   he has a good case er hat ein gutes
   Argument
   see **special**
cash das Bargeld
   I haven't any cash ich habe kein Bargeld
   will you cash a cheque for me? können Sie
   mir einen Scheck einlösen?
cash desk die Kasse

....

cash flow der Cash-flow, die Liquidität
cash flow forecast die Liquiditätsprognose
cash flow problems Liquiditätsprobleme
  because of cash flow problems wegen
  finanzieller Engpässe
cassette eine Cassette
catch: where do we catch the bus? wo fährt
  der Bus ab?
cater for: to cater for your special needs um
  Ihre besonderen Wünsche zu berücksichtigen
cause: the cause of the trouble die Ursache des
  Problems
  the main cause der Hauptgrund
  it's caused a bit of inconvenience es hat
  schon einige Unannehmlichkeiten bereitet
ceiling (*Fin: limit*) die Grenze
  up to a ceiling of ... bis zu einer Grenze von ...
cellophane das Cellophan
centigrade Celsius
» *to convert C to F* : $\frac{C}{5} \times 9 + 32 = F$

centigrade	−10	−5	0	10	15	21	30	36.9
Fahrenheit	14	23	32	50	59	70	86	98.4

centimetre ein Zentimeter
» *1 cm = 0.39 inches*
central zentral
centre das Zentrum
  how do we get to the centre? wie kommen
  wir zur Stadtmitte?
certain bestimmt
  are you certain? sind Sie sicher?
  we're certain that ... wir sind sicher, daß ...
  please make certain that ... bitte prüfen Sie
  nach, ob ...
  I'll make certain (*check*) ich prüfe es nach

ä [eh], au as in h*ow*, äu, eu [oy], ei as in I, ie [ee]
ö as in h*er*, ü, y as in h*u*ge, -b [-p], -d [-t], j [y], qu [kv]
s- [z-], ß [ss], v [f], w [v], z [ts]

....

certificate eine Bescheinigung
certificate of insurance der
  Versicherungsschein, die Police
chainstore ein Kettenladen
chair der Stuhl
  (*armchair*) der Sessel
  to be in the chair (*at meeting*) den Vorsitz
  führen
chairman der Vorsitzende
chairperson der/die Vorsitzende
chambermaid das Zimmermädchen
chamber of commerce die Handelskammer
champagne der Sekt
chance: just one more chance nur noch eine
  Chance
  it's an excellent chance to ... es ist eine
  ausgezeichnete Gelegenheit, um zu ...
change: there are going to be a lot of changes
  es wird sich vieles ändern
  three more changes to the contract/
  specifications noch drei Änderungen am
  Vertrag/in den Angaben
  keep us informed of any changes in the
  situation halten Sie uns auf dem laufenden
  I haven't any change ich habe kein
  Kleingeld
  could you change this into marks? können
  Sie das bitte in D-Mark umtauschen?
  do we have to change trains? müssen wir
  umsteigen?
  I'd like to change my booking/flight etc ich
  möchte umbuchen
  it can't be changed now es kann jetzt nicht
  mehr geändert werden
  a lot of people are changing to ... viele Leute
  wechseln jetzt zu ... über
channel: the Channel der Ärmelkanal
charge: what do you charge? was verlangen
  Sie?

what are the charges? wie hoch sind die
Gebühren?
no extra charge kein Aufpreis
who's in charge? wer hat die Verantwortung?
charge it up stellen Sie es in Rechnung
we have charged it to your account wir
haben es Ihnen in Rechnung gestellt
who do I charge it to? wem soll ich das
berechnen?
chart (*flow chart etc*) ein Diagramm
chartered accountant der Wirtschaftsprüfer
cheap billig
check: detailed checks have shown that ...
genaue Überprüfungen haben gezeigt, daß ...
regular checks will be carried out es
werden regelmäßige Kontrollen durchgeführt
will you check? bitte prüfen Sie das nach
I've checked ich habe es nachgeprüft
will you check the total? können Sie bitte die
Endsumme überprüfen?
we checked in/we checked out wir haben
uns angemeldet/abgemeldet
have you checked your facts? haben Sie
Ihre Angaben genau überprüft?
I'll check it out ich werde das überprüfen
(*find out*) ich seh mal nach
checklist die Checkliste
chef der Koch
chemist's die Drogerie
(*dispensing*) die Apotheke
cheque der Scheck
will you take a cheque? nehmen Sie
Schecks?
cheque book das Scheckbuch

ä [eh], au as in h*ow*, äu, eu [oy], ei as in I, ie [ee]
ö as in h*er*, ü, y as in h*u*ge, -b [-p], -d [-t], j [y], qu [kv]
s- [z-], ß [ss], v [f], w [v], z [ts]

....

cheque card die Scheckkarte
chest die Brust
children die Kinder
chocolate die Schokolade
choice: a wider choice of products eine
   größere Auswahl an Produkten
   we have no choice es bleibt uns keine andere
   Wahl
choose auswählen
Christian name der Vorname
» *TRAVEL TIP: use of Christian names is not*
   standard practice in business; best to let the
   German speaker take the initiative
Christmas Weihnachten
cider der Apfelmost
c.i.f. cif [sif]
cigar die Zigarre
cigarette die Zigarette
cinema das Kino
circular das Rundschreiben
circumstances: under no circumstances
   unter keinen Umständen
   in the circumstances unter diesen
   Umständen
city die Stadt
   the City die (Londoner) City
claim: our claim against the carrier unser
   Anspruch an die Transportfirma
   the claims we make for our products die
   Eigenschaften, die wir unseren Produkten
   zuschreiben
   we intend to claim damages wir wollen
   Anspruch auf Schadenersatz erheben
clarification die Klarstellung
clarify klarstellen
clean sauber
clear klar
   I'm not clear about it ich bin mir darüber
   nicht im klaren

I want to make this perfectly clear ich möchte das ein für alle Mal klarstellen
I'd be grateful if you would clear it up ich wäre Ihnen für eine Klarstellung dankbar
when they're cleared through Customs nach der Zollabfertigung
clearance (*customs*) die Zollabfertigung
clearing bank die Clearingbank
clerical error ein Versehen
clerk der/die kaufmännische Angestellte
clever klug
client der Klient
cloakroom die Garderobe; (*WC*) die Toilette
clock die Uhr
close[1] nah
close[2]: **when do you close?** wann machen Sie zu?
closed geschlossen
close down (*business*) stillegen
they've closed down sie haben zugemacht
cloth das Tuch
clothes die Kleidung
co- Ko-, ko-
c/o bei, c/o
coach der Bus
coat der Mantel
c.o.d. per Nachnahme
coffee ein Kaffee
    white coffee/black coffee Kaffee mit Milch/ schwarzer Kaffee
    two coffees, please zwei Kaffee, bitte
    YOU MAY THEN HEAR ...
    Kännchen oder Tassen? *pots or cups?*
    a pot is usually 2 cups; coffee and cream are always served separately

---

ä [eh], au as in h*ow*, äu, eu [oy], ei as in I, ie [ee]
ö as in h*er*, ü, y as in h*uge*, -b [-p], -d [-t], j [y], qu [kv]
s- [z-], ß [ss], v [f], w [v], z [ts]

coin die Münze
coincidence der Zufall
cold kalt
  I've got a cold ich bin erkältet
collaboration die Zusammenarbeit
collar der Kragen
colleague der Kollege/die Kollegin
collect abholen
  see **reverse**
collection (*of debts*) die Einziehung
  bill for collection ein Inkassowechsel
colour die Farbe
  have you any other colours? haben Sie das
  noch in anderen Farben?
comb ein Kamm
come kommen
  I come from London ich komme aus London
  we came here yesterday wir sind gestern
  hier angekommen
  when is he coming? wann kommt er?
  come on! kommen Sie!
  if we come to an agreement falls wir zu einer
  Übereinkunft kommen
  when are you next coming to see us? wann
  kommen Sie das nächste Mal zu uns?
comfortable bequem
comments Kommentare
  do you have any comments? haben Sie noch
  Kommentare dazu?
commerce der Handel
commercial kommerziell
commission die Provision
  on a commission basis auf Provision(sbasis)
commission agent der Kommissionär, der
  Provisionsvertreter
commit: we're fully committed to this project
  wir haben uns in dieser Sache vollkommen
  festgelegt
  we've committed a lot of time/money to

this project wir haben in diese Sache viel
Zeit/Geld investiert
you don't have to commit yourself Sie
brauchen sich nicht festzulegen
I can't commit myself now ich kann mich
jetzt noch nicht festlegen
commitment: our financial commitments
unsere finanziellen Verpflichtungen
committee das Komitee
committee meeting die Ausschußsitzung
Common Market die EG [ay-gay]
commute pendeln
company die Firma
company car der Firmenwagen
company policy die Firmenpolitik
company report der Firmenbericht
company secretary der Company Secretary
compare vergleichen
as compared with last year im Vergleich
zum Vorjahr
compensation die Entschädigung
I demand compensation ich verlange
Schadenersatz
compete konkurrieren
we can't compete with these prices wir
können mit diesen Preisen nicht mithalten
competent kompetent
I'm not competent to deal with that ich
fühle mich in dieser Angelegenheit nicht
kompetent
competition die Konkurrenz
strong competition große Konkurrenz
competitive *(prices, product)* konkurrenzfähig
competitors: our competitors unsere
Konkurrenten

ä [eh], au as in h*ow*, äu, eu [oy], ei as in I, ie [ee]
ö as in h*er*, ü, y as in h*u*ge, -b [-p], -d [-t], j [y], qu [kv]
s- [z-], ß [ss], v [f], w [v], z [ts]

complain sich beschweren
complaint die Beschwerde
complete: is work complete? ist die Arbeit
abgeschlossen?
 the complete range das komplette Angebot
completely völlig
completion: on completion of the work nach
Abschluß der Arbeit
complicated: it's very complicated es ist sehr
kompliziert
compliment das Kompliment
 my compliments to the chef ein Lob der
Küche
**comply: in order to comply with your
requests ...** um Ihren Wünschen zu
entsprechen
 it doesn't comply with ... das entspricht
nicht ...
component ein Bestandteil, eine Komponente
computer der Computer
computerized computerisiert
**concern: we are very concerned to hear
that ...** wir sind sehr beunruhigt, daß ...
 as far as we are concerned was uns betrifft
 concerning your letter bezüglich Ihres
Schreibens
concession die Konzession
concessionaire der Konzessionär
conclusion: what's your conclusion? zu
welchem Schluß sind Sie gekommen?
 we must draw the appropriate conclusions
wir müssen die entsprechenden Schlüsse
ziehen
conclusive endgültig
condition die Bedingung
 it's not in very good condition es ist nicht in
besonders gutem Zustand
conditional acceptance Annahme mit
Vorbehalt

conference die Konferenz
conference room (*in hotel*) der Konferenzraum
confidence das Vertrauen
confidential vertraulich
 this is strictly confidential das ist streng
 vertraulich
confirm bestätigen
confirmation die Bestätigung
 we look forward to receiving confirmation
 wir sehen dem Erhalt Ihrer Bestätigung mit
 Interesse entgegen
confirmed letter of credit bestätigter
 Kreditbrief
conformity die Übereinstimmung
 it is not in conformity with ... das entspricht
 nicht ...
confuse: you're confusing me Sie bringen
 mich durcheinander
congratulations! herzlichen Glückwunsch!
connection die Verbindung
connoisseur der Kenner
conscious bewußt
consent: do we have your consent? können
 wir mit Ihrer Zustimmung rechnen?
consequence die Konsequenz
 as a consequence of this als Folge davon
consider: we are considering it wir befassen
 uns damit
 please ask him to consider it bitten Sie ihn,
 das zu überdenken
 have you considered making any changes?
 haben Sie über eventuelle Änderungen
 nachgedacht?
 it's worth considering es ist eine Überlegung
 wert

ä [eh], au as in h*ow*, äu, eu [oy], ei as in I, ie [ee]
ö as in h*er*, ü, y as in h*u*ge, -b [-p], -d [-t], j [y], qu [kv]
s- [z-], ß [ss], v [f], w [v], z [ts]

considering its age in Anbetracht seines Alters

all things considered wenn man alles in Betracht zieht

consideration: on consideration of ... mit Rücksicht auf ...

after due consideration nach reichlicher Überlegung

consignee der Empfänger

consigner der Versender

consignment die Sendung, die Ladung

consignment note der Frachtbrief

consul der Konsul

consulate das Konsulat

consult: I have to consult with ... ich muß mich mit ... beraten

consultancy die Beratung *(agency)* das Beratungsbüro

consultant der Berater

consultation die Beratung

consumer der Verbraucher

consumer needs die Verbraucherbedürfnisse

contact: a useful contact ein nützlicher Kontakt

how can I contact ...? wie kann ich ... erreichen?

I'll get in contact soon ich werde mich bald melden

please do not hesitate to contact us setzen Sie sich jederzeit mit uns in Verbindung

contacts Beziehungen

container der Container

container base der Containerterminal

contract der Vertrag

under the terms of the contract unter den Vertragsbedingungen

contribution *(to project etc)* der Beitrag

control: under our control unter unserer Kontrolle

the necessary management control die nötige Kontrolle von oben
due to circumstances beyond our control aufgrund von unvorhergesehenen Umständen
controlling factor der beherrschende Faktor
convenience: at your earliest convenience möglichst bald
convenient günstig
conviction die Überzeugung
convince: I want to convince you that ... ich möchte Sie davon überzeugen, daß ...
cook: it's not cooked es ist nicht gar
it was beautifully cooked das war vorzüglich
cool kühl
cooperate zusammenarbeiten
cooperation die Zusammenarbeit
cooperative kooperativ
coordinate koordinieren
cope: can you cope with that? werden Sie damit fertig?
copy: 3 copies drei Exemplare
we'll send you a copy wir senden Ihnen ein Exemplar zu
please copy head office bitte ein Exemplar an die Zentrale
corner die Ecke
can we have a corner table? können wir einen Ecktisch haben?
to corner the market Monopolstellung erreichen
correct richtig
correspond to entsprechen
correspondence die Korrespondenz
cost: what does it cost? was kostet das?
our costs unsere Kosten

ä [eh], au as in h*ow*, äu, eu [oy], ei as in I, ie [ee]
ö as in h*er*, ü, y as in h*uge*, -b [-p], -d [-t], j [y], qu [kv]
s- [z-], ß [ss], v [f], w [v], z [ts]

....

at cost zum Selbstkostenpreis
it's been carefully costed es wurde genau
kalkuliert
cost analysis die Kostenanalyse
cost-conscious kostenbewußt
cost-effective kosteneffizient
cost estimate der Kostenvoranschlag
costing die Kalkulation
cost price der Selbstkostenpreis
cotton die Baumwolle
cotton wool die Watte
couchette der Liegesitz
could: could you please ...? könnten Sie
bitte ...?
could I have ...? könnte ich bitte ... haben?
we couldn't ... wir konnten nicht ...
country das Land
in the country auf dem Land
couple: a couple of ... ein paar ...
courier (*express*) der Kurier
by courier per Kurier
course: in the course of the meeting im
Verlauf der Besprechung
in the course of the next 3 months im Lauf
der nächsten drei Monate
of course natürlich
court: I'll take you to court ich werde Sie vor
Gericht bringen
cover: to cover our costs um unsere Kosten zu
decken
insurance cover die Versicherungsdeckung
cover charge ein Gedeck
covering letter der Begleitbrief
crate eine Kiste
crazy verrückt
credit der Kredit
(*on statement*) Guthaben
we are in credit wir haben Geld auf dem
Konto

to the credit of your account Ihrem Konto
zur Gutschrift
**the bank is willing to grant us credit/
extend our credit** die Bank ist bereit, uns ein
Darlehen zu gewähren/unser Darlehen zu
verlängern
on the credit side auf der Habenseite
please credit to the following account ...
bitte schreiben Sie dem folgenden Konto ... gut
we are today crediting to you the sum of ...
wir überweisen Ihnen heute den Betrag von ...
credit card die Kreditkarte
credit facilities Kreditmöglichkeiten
credit limit die Kreditgrenze
credit note eine Gutschrift
creditor der Gläubiger
credit references Kreditreferenzen
credit terms Kreditbedingungen
credit-worthy kreditwürdig
crisis die Krise
critical path der kritische Pfad
criticism die Kritik
we have one criticism einen Punkt müssen
wir kritisieren
criticize kritisieren
**cross: our letters must have crossed in the
post** unsere Schreiben müssen sich gekreuzt
haben
cumulative kumulativ
cup die Tasse
a cup of coffee eine Tasse Kaffee
currency die Währung
current derzeitig
(*month*) laufend
current account das Kontokorrentkonto

ä [eh], au as in h*ow*, äu, eu [oy], ei as in I, ie [ee]
ö as in h*er*, ü, y as in h*uge*, -b [-p], -d [-t], j [y], qu [kv]
s- [z-], ß [ss], v [f], w [v], z [ts]

current assets das Umlaufvermögen
current earnings die laufenden Einnahmen
current liabilities kurzfristige
 Verbindlichkeiten
curriculum vitae der Lebenslauf
customer der Kunde
customer complaint eine Kundenbeschwerde
customer service der Kundendienst
Customs der Zoll
Customs Authorities die Zollbehörden
Customs clearance die Zollabfertigung
Customs duty der Zoll
cut: job cuts Stellenstreichungen
 there have been cuts all round es sind
 überall Einsparungen durchgeführt worden
 to cut costs Kosten verringern
cutback die Einsparung
Czech tschechisch
Czechoslovakia die Tschechoslowakei
damage: we'll pay for the damage wir werden
 für den Schaden aufkommen
 it's damaged es ist beschädigt
 damaged in transit auf dem Transport
 beschädigt
damages der Schadenersatz
 they are claiming damages sie erheben
 Anspruch auf Schadenersatz
Damen ladies
dangerous gefährlich
Danish dänisch
dark dunkel
Darlehen loan
data Daten
data processing die Datenverarbeitung
date: what's the date? der Wievielte ist heute?
 can we fix a date? können wir einen Termin
 ausmachen?
 on the fifth of May am fünften Mai
 date of invoicing das Rechnungsdatum

to date we have not ... bis heute haben wir noch nicht ...

in 1984 neunzehnhundertvierundachtzig

» *to say the date in German add letters 'ten' to the number if 1–19, and 'sten' if 20–31; see numbers on p 188-189; exceptions:* **first** ersten; **third** dritten; **seventh** siebten

day der Tag

DDR [day-day-air] =*Deutsche Demokratische Republik GDR, German Democratic Republic*

dead tot

deadline eine Frist

if we make/miss the deadline falls wir die Frist einhalten/nicht einhalten

deadlock eine Pattsituation

deal: we made a deal wir haben ein Geschäft gemacht

it's a deal abgemacht

I'll make a deal with you ich schlage Ihnen ein Geschäft vor

will you deal with it? kümmern Sie sich bitte darum?

we don't deal in... wir handeln nicht mit ...

dealer der Händler

dealership die Franchise

dear (*expensive*) teuer

Dear Mr Kunz Sehr geehrter Herr Kunz

Dear Franz Lieber Franz

Dear Sir(s) Sehr geehrte Damen und Herren

see **letter**

debatable fraglich

debentures Obligationen

debit (*on statement*) das Soll

a debit of £1,000 ein Soll von £1.000

on the debit side auf der Sollseite

ä [eh], au as in h*ow*, äu, eu [oy], ei as in I, ie [ee]
ö as in h*er*, ü, y as in h*uge*, -b [-p], -d [-t], j [y], qu [kv]
s- [z-], ß [ss], v [f], w [v], z [ts]

....

we have debited you with... wir haben Ihr Konto mit ... belastet
please debit our account bitte belasten Sie unser Konto
debt die Schuld
debtor der Schuldner
December Dezember
decide: we have decided to... wir haben beschlossen, ... zu ...
we've decided on... wir haben uns für ... entschieden
that hasn't been decided yet das ist noch nicht entschieden
decision die Entscheidung
we need a decision today wir brauchen noch heute eine Entscheidung
if we reach/make a decision falls wir eine Entscheidung treffen
decision-maker der Entscheidungsträger
declare: nothing to declare nichts zu verzollen
decrease *(in sales etc)* ein Rückgang
deep tief
defect der Fehler
defective fehlerhaft
deficit das Defizit
defendant der/die Angeklagte *(in civil cases)* der/die Beklagte
definite definitiv
it's not definite yet das ist noch nicht sicher
definitely bestimmt
definitely not bestimmt nicht
delay *(in production etc)* die Verzögerung
the flight was delayed die Maschine hatte Verspätung
deliberately absichtlich
delicate *(situation)* heikel
delicious köstlich
deliver: when can you deliver? wann können Sie liefern?

delivery: what sort of delivery are you looking for? welche Lieferzeit erwarten Sie?
to take delivery of something etwas in Empfang nehmen
is there another mail delivery? gibt es noch eine Zustellung?
delivery date der Liefertermin
delivery deadline die Lieferfrist
de luxe Luxus-
demand (*for goods*) die Nachfrage
(not) in demand (nicht) gefragt
demonstration (*of gadget*) eine Vorführung
Denmark Dänemark
dentist der Zahnarzt
deny: I deny it das bestreite ich
department store das Kaufhaus
departure die Abreise
(*bus, train*) die Abfahrt
(*plane*) der Abflug
depend: it depends das kommt darauf an
it depends on him das kommt auf ihn an
you can depend on it Sie können sich darauf verlassen
deposit die Kaution
do I have to leave a deposit? muß ich eine Kaution hinterlegen?
deposit account das Sparkonto
depot das Depot
depreciation (*of goods*) die Wertminderung
(*on balance sheet*) Abschreibungen
depressed (*market*) flau
describe beschreiben
description die Beschreibung
desirable: it would be desirable if ... es wäre wünschenswert, wenn ...

ä [eh], au as in how, äu, eu [oy], ei as in I, ie [ee]
ö as in her, ü, y as in huge, -b [-p], -d [-t], j [y], qu [kv]
s- [z-], ß [ss], v [f], w [v], z [ts]

dessert der Nachtisch
destination das Ziel
  (*of goods*) der Bestimmungsort
detail die Einzelheit
  let's discuss the details wir wollen die
  Einzelheiten besprechen
  I want to study this in detail ich möchte
  mich ganz genau damit befassen
  a detailed report ein detaillierter Bericht
Detailhändler retailer
detour der Umweg
*Deutsche Demokratische Republik German
  Democratic Republic*
devalued abgewertet
develop entwickeln
  (*a business*) ausbauen
  a developing market ein wachsender Markt
development (*of business*) die
  (Geschäfts)entwicklung
  a recent development eine neuere
  Entwicklung
  an unexpected development eine
  unvorhergesehene Entwicklung
development grant eine Entwicklungsbeihilfe
Devisen foreign exchange
d.h.=das heißt i.e.
diagram das Diagramm
dialling code die Vorwahl
diamond der Diamant
diarrhoea der Durchfall
diary der Terminkalender
  I've got it in my diary es steht in meinem
  Terminkalender
dictating machine ein Diktiergerät
dictionary das Wörterbuch
diesel (*fuel*) Diesel
diet die Diät
  I'm on a diet ich mache eine Schlankheitskur
difference der Unterschied

the price difference der Preisunterschied
**the main difference with our arrangement
is...** der wesentliche Unterschied bei unserer
Vereinbarung ist ...
it doesn't make any difference das ist egal
different: they are different sie sind
verschieden
can I have a different room? kann ich ein
anderes Zimmer haben?
is there a different route? gibt es eine andere
Strecke?
differently anders
difficult schwierig
difficulty die Schwierigkeit
we're having difficulties with... wir haben
Schwierigkeiten mit ...
DIN [deen] = *Deutsche Industrie-Normen
equivalent of British Standards*
dining room (*in hotel*) der Speiseraum
dinner das Abendessen
dinner jacket die Smokingjacke
direct direkt
does it go direct? ist es eine Direkt-
verbindung?
if they want to buy direct from us wenn sie
direkt von uns kaufen wollen
direction die Richtung
the direction in which things are moving
wie sich die Dinge entwickeln
follow the directions befolgen Sie die
Anweisungen
director der Direktor
dirty schmutzig
disadvantage der Nachteil
disappear verschwinden

ä [eh], au as in h*ow*, äu, eu [oy], ei as in I, ie [ee]
ö as in h*er*, ü, y as in h*uge*, -b [-p], -d [-t], j [y], qu [kv]
s- [z-], ß [ss], v [f], w [v], z [ts]

....

disappointing enttäuschend
disco die Disko
discount der Rabatt
   (*settlement discount*) Skonto
discreet: please be discreet seien Sie bitte
   diskret
discrepancy eine Diskrepanz
discretion: we'll leave it to your discretion
   wir stellen es in Ihr Ermessen
   at your discretion in Ihrem Ermessen
   discretion is called for Diskretion erwünscht
discuss diskutieren
discussion die Diskussion
dishonest unehrlich
dispatch versenden
   they'll be ready for dispatch sie sind
   versandfertig
dispatch date der Liefertermin
dispatch note der Begleitschein
display pack das Display, die Display-Packung
distance die Entfernung
   in the distance in der Ferne
distribution der Vertrieb
distribution network das Vertriebsnetz
distribution rights Vertriebsrechte
distributor der Vertriebshändler
   (*wholesaler*) der Großhändler
distributor discount Händlerrabatt
distributorship die Konzession
disturb: the noise is disturbing me der Lärm
   stört mich
dividend die Dividende
divorced geschieden
do machen
   how do you do? guten Tag/Abend
   what are you doing tonight? was machen
   Sie heute abend?
   how do you do it? wie machen Sie das?
   it won't do das geht nicht

I've never done it before das habe ich noch
nie gemacht
we're doing everything we can wir tun
unser möglichstes
what are you doing about it? was
unternehmen Sie da?
docket der Warenbegleitschein
docks die Docks
doctor der Arzt
I need a doctor ich brauche einen Arzt
document das Dokument
documentary credit der Dokumentarkredit,
das Dokumentenakkreditiv
documentation die Dokumentation
Dokumentenakkreditiv documentary credit
dollar der Dollar
domestic (*trade, market etc*) Binnen-
door die Tür
Doppelsteuerabkommen reciprocal taxation
agreement
double: **double room** ein Doppelzimmer
double whisky ein doppelter Whisky
at double the price zum doppelten Preis
double check: **I'll double-check** ich
(über)prüfe es noch einmal
will you double-check? (über)prüfen Sie es
bitte noch einmal
down unten
sales are down on last year der Verkauf ist
gegenüber dem Vorjahr zurückgegangen
sales are down 15% der Verkauf ist um
fünfzehn Prozent zurückgegangen
to keep/get costs down die Kosten niedrig
halten
downmarket wenig anspruchsvoll

ä [eh], au as in h*ow*, äu, eu [oy], ei as in I, ie [ee]
ö as in h*er*, ü, y as in h*u*ge, -b [-p], -d [-t], j [y], qu [kv]
s- [z-], ß [ss], v [f], w [v], z [ts]

down payment eine Anzahlung
dozen ein Dutzend
draft (*of contract etc*) ein Entwurf
   the draft agreement der Vertragsentwurf
drastic drastisch
draw (*money*) abheben
   a bill drawn on... ein Wechsel auf ...
   ausgestellt
drawback der Nachteil
drawee der Bezogene
drawer der Aussteller
drawing (*plan etc*) der Plan
draw up (*documents*) aufsetzen
   incorrectly drawn up falsch aufgesetzt
dress das Kleid
drink: would you like a drink? möchten Sie
   etwas trinken?
   I don't drink ich trinke keinen Alkohol
drive: you drive a hard bargain Sie stellen ja
   harte Forderungen
   I've been driving all day ich bin den ganzen
   Tag gefahren
driver der Fahrer
driving licence der Führerschein
» *TRAVEL TIP: driving in Germany; speed
limits: 50 kph (31 mph) in town; 100 (62)
outside; motorways 130 (81) recommended
with 60 (37) minimum; trucks max. 80 (49);
driving on side lights illegal; seat belt, red
triangle and first aid kit compulsory*
drop: a drop in sales/output ein Rückgang im
   Verkauf/in der Produktion
drücken *push*
drunk betrunken
dry trocken
dry-clean chemisch reinigen
dry-cleaner die Reinigung
due: when is the train due? wann soll der Zug
   ankommen?

the next payment is due on... die nächste
Zahlung ist am ... fällig
it falls due... es ist am ... fällig
due to wegen
in due course zu gegebener Zeit
Durchfahrt verboten no through road
Durchgangsverkehr through traffic
Durchschlag carbon copy
during während
Duschen showers
Dutch holländisch
dutiable zollpflichtig
duty (*import*) Einfuhrzoll
duty-free goods zollfreie Ware
dynamic dynamisch
each: can we have one each? können wir jeder
eins haben?
how much are they each? was kosten sie pro
Stück?
early früh
we want to leave a day earlier wir möchten
einen Tag früher abreisen
next month at the earliest frühestens
nächsten Monat
east der Osten
Easter Ostern
East German DDR- [day-day-air]
East Germany die DDR
» *TRAVEL TIP: a visa is necessary both for entry
(Einreise) and exit (Ausreise); letter of
invitation or telex from GDR business contact is
necessary in order to obtain visa; register with
police within 24 hours of arrival and then exit
visa and residence permit (Aufenthalts-
genehmigung) will be issued; some bigger*

ä [eh], au as in h*ow*, äu, eu [oy], ei as in I, ie [ee]
ö as in h*er*, ü, y as in h*u*ge, -b [-p], -d [-t], j [y], qu [kv]
s- [z-], ß [ss], v [f], w [v], z [ts]

....

hotels will do this for you; GDR currency may
not be changed back into non-GDR currency;
further information from GDR Embassy
easy leicht
eat: something to eat etwas zu essen
economic wirtschaftlich
economic forecast die Wirtschaftsprognose
economy: the economy die Wirtschaft
EDV [ay-day-fow] = *elektronische*
  Datenverarbeitung EDP
EEC die EG [ay-gay]
EEC subsidies EG-Beihilfen
effect (*consequence*) die Auswirkung
  it comes into effect es tritt in Kraft
  with immediate effect mit sofortiger
  Wirkung
  with effect as of next month ab nächsten
  Monat wirksam
  no longer in effect außer Kraft
effective (*measures*) wirksam
effectively (*in effect*) effektiv
efficiency die Effizienz
efficient effizient
effort die Mühe
  thank you for your efforts vielen Dank für
  Ihre Mühe
  we shall spare no effort wir werden keine
  Mühe scheuen
EFTA die EFTA
EG [ay-gay] *EEC*
Einbahnstraße one-way street
Einfahrt entrance (to motorway)
Einfuhr import
Eingang entrance
einordnen *get in lane*
Einschreiben registered
Einstieg vorn/hinten enter at the front/rear
Eintritt frei admission free
Einzelhandel retail

Eire Ireland
either: either ... or ... entweder ... oder
  I don't like either mir gefällt beides nicht
elastic elastisch
elastic band ein Gummiband
electric elektrisch
electrician der Elektriker
electricity die Elektrizität
» *TRAVEL TIP: voltage is 220 AC*
electronic elektronisch
elegant elegant
else: something else etwas anderes
  somewhere else irgendwo anders
  let's go somewhere else gehen wir woanders
  hin
  who else? wer sonst?
  or else sonst
embarrassed verlegen
embarrassing peinlich
embassy die Botschaft
emergency der Notfall
Empfänger consignee; recipient
emphasis: we put the emphasis on ... wir
  legen besonderen Wert auf ...
emphasize betonen
employee der Arbeitnehmer
employer der Arbeitgeber
employment: the people in your employment
  Ihre Angestellten
  to create employment Stellen schaffen
empty leer
enclose: I enclose ... ich füge ... bei
enclosed: please find enclosed ... anbei
  übersenden wir Ihnen ...
  the enclosed cheque beiliegender Scheck

ä [eh], au as in h*ow*, äu, eu [oy], ei as in I, ie [ee]
ö as in h*er*, ü, y as in h*uge*, -b [-p], -d [-t], j [y], qu [kv]
s- [z-], ß [ss], v [f], w [v], z [ts]

....

end das Ende
  when does it end? bis wann geht es?
engagement: a prior engagement ein bereits
  ausgemachter Termin
engine die Maschine
  (*of car, plane*) der Motor
engineer der Ingenieur; der Techniker
engineering die Technologie
  very advanced engineering fortschrittliche
  Technologie
  some engineering problems einige
  technische Probleme
England England
English englisch
  the English die Engländer
  I'm English ich bin Engländer
  (*woman*) ich bin Engländerin
enormous enorm
enough genug
  thank you, that's enough danke, das genügt
enquire: I'll enquire ich erkundige mich
enquiry die Anfrage
  could you make enquiries? könnten Sie sich
  bitte erkundigen?
ensure sicherstellen
  please ensure that ... stellen Sie bitte sicher,
  daß ...
entail zur Folge haben
  this will entail ... das hat ... zur Folge
entertainment die Unterhaltung
entitle berechtigen
  you will be entitled to ... Sie sind zu ...
  berechtigt
Entladung off-loading
entrance der Eingang
entry der Eintritt
entry permit (*for GDR*) der Passierschein
  » *TRAVEL TIP: see* **East Germany**
envelope der Umschlag

envisage sich etwas vorstellen
  do you envisage any changes? halten Sie
  eventuelle Änderungen für wahrscheinlich?
equipment die Ausrüstung
  electrical equipment Elektrogeräte
equity (*capital*) das Eigenkapital
equivalent: that is the equivalent of ... das
  entspricht ...
  or any equivalent method oder eine
  entsprechende Methode
Erdgeschoß ground floor
Erfrischungen refreshments
error der Fehler
  sent to you in error aus Versehen an Sie
  geschickt
Erste Hilfe first aid
Erwachsene adults
especially besonders
essential notwendig
  it is essential that ... es ist unbedingt
  erforderlich, daß ...
establish: we have established that ... (*found*
  out) wir haben herausgefunden, daß ...
estimate die Schätzung
  (*of costs*) der Kostenvoranschlag
  what's your estimate? was veranschlagen
  Sie?
  we estimate that ... wir schätzen, daß ...
  estimated costs veranschlagte Kosten
  sales estimate die Absatzkalkulation
ETA geschätzte Ankunft
Etat budget
Europe Europa
European europäisch
even: even the British sogar die Briten

ä [eh], au as in h*ow*, äu, eu [oy], ei as in I, ie [ee]
ö as in h*er*, ü, y as in h*u*ge, -b [-p], -d [-t], j [y], qu [kv]
s- [z-], ß [ss], v [f], w [v], z [ts]

....

evening der Abend
  good evening guten Abend
  this evening heute abend
evening dress der Abendanzug
  (*woman's*) das Abendkleid
ever: have you ever been to ...? waren Sie
  schon einmal in ...?
every jede(r, s)
everyone jeder
  is everyone here? sind alle da?
everything alles
  everything we've tried alles, was wir
  versucht haben
everywhere überall
evidence der Beweis
exact(ly) genau
exaggerate übertreiben
example das Beispiel
  for example zum Beispiel
exceed übersteigen
  not exceeding £500 nicht über £500
excellent ausgezeichnet
except außer
  except me außer mir
exception eine Ausnahme
  as an exception ausnahmsweise
  we can't make any exceptions wir können
  keine Ausnahme machen
excess baggage das Übergewicht
excess fare der Zuschlag
exchange (*for money*) die Wechselstube
  (*telephone*) das Fernamt
  a useful exchange of ideas ein wertvoller
  Gedankenaustausch
exchange rate der Wechselkurs
exciting (*idea*) hochinteressant
excuse: excuse me entschuldigen Sie bitte
  I offer no excuses ich will mich nicht
  entschuldigen

executive ein leitender Angestellter
executive case der Aktenkoffer
ex factory ab Fabrik
ex gratia payment eine Sonderzahlung
exhausted erschöpft
exhibition die Ausstellung
exhibitor der Aussteller
exit der Ausgang
expect erwarten
  we didn't expect that das haben wir nicht
  erwartet
  larger than expected größer als erwartet
expenditure die Ausgaben
expense die Kosten
  at your/our expense auf Ihre/unsere Kosten
  it's on expenses das geht auf Spesen
expense account das Spesenkonto
expensive teuer
experience die Erfahrung
  in our experience unserer Erfahrung nach
experienced erfahren
experimental: an experimental model ein
  Versuchsmodell
  on an experimental basis auf Probebasis
expert der Experte
expire: it expires next month es läuft nächsten
  Monat ab
expiry der Ablauf
  the expiry of the contract der Vertrags-
  ablauf
expiry date das Verfalldatum, der Verfallstag
explain erklären
  would you explain that slowly? können Sie
  das bitte langsam erklären?
explanation die Erklärung

ä [eh], au as in h*ow*, äu, eu [oy], ei as in I, ie [ee]
ö as in h*er*, ü, y as in h*u*ge, -b [-p], -d [-t], j [y], qu [kv]
s- [z-], ß [ss], v [f], w [v], z [ts]

export der Export
  (*verb*) exportieren
export director der Exportdirektor
export documents die Exportdokumente
export drive die Exportkampagne
export licence die Exportlizenz
export manager der Exportmanager
express (*send letter*) per Expreß, per Eilboten
extend verlängern
extension die Verlängerung
extra extra
  an extra cost/month zusätzliche Kosten/ein
  zusätzlicher Monat
  is that extra? wird das extra berechnet?
extremely äußerst
ex warehouse ab Lager
ex works ab Werk
Fa.=Firma firm
Fabrik factory
face das Gesicht
facility die Einrichtung
  we don't have the facilities to ... wir haben
  keine Einrichtungen, um ... zu ...
fact die Tatsache
fact-finding tour die Informationsreise
factor der Faktor
factory die Fabrik
factsheet das Informationsblatt
Fahrenheit
» *to convert F to C:* $F-32\times\dfrac{5}{9}=C$

Fahrenheit	14	23	32	50	59	70	86	98.4
centigrade	−10	−5	0	10	15	21	30	36.9

Fahrkarten tickets
fail: if we fail to meet the target falls wir das
  gesteckte Ziel nicht erreichen
failing: failing that wenn das nicht möglich ist
failure der Mißerfolg

failure rate die Mißerfolgsquote
fair fair
   (*commercial*) die Messe
   that's not fair das ist nicht fair
faithfully: **yours faithfully** Mit freundlichen
   Grüßen
   see **letter**
fake eine Fälschung
fall fallen
   he's fallen er ist hingefallen
   prices/sales are falling die Preise fallen/der
   Absatz geht zurück
   falling demand/interest rates
   zurückgehende Nachfrage/fallende Zinsen
   output fell to ... der Umsatz ging auf ... zurück
   we can always fall back on ... wir können
   stets auf ... zurückgreifen
fällig due
Fälligkeit maturity
Fälligkeitstag maturity date
false falsch
famous berühmt
fan der Ventilator
far weit
   is it far? ist es weit?
   how far is it? wie weit ist es?
fare (*travel*) der Fahrpreis
   (*on plane*) der Flugpreis
far-fetched weithergeholt
f.a.s. frei Kai
fascinating faszinierend
fashion die Mode
fast schnell
   don't speak so fast sprechen Sie bitte nicht so
   schnell!

ä [eh], au as in h*ow*, äu, eu [oy], ei as in I, ie [ee]
ö as in h*er*, ü, y as in h*u*ge, -b [-p], -d [-t], j [y], qu [kv]
     s- [z-], ß [ss], v [f], w [v], z [ts]

fault der Fehler
  it's not our fault das ist nicht unsere Schuld
faulty defekt
favour: **credit in your/our favour** Guthaben zu
  Ihren/unseren Gunsten
  I'm in favour ich bin dafür
  we would favour ... wir würden ... vorziehen
favourable (*conditions, terms*) günstig
  we look forward to a favourable reply wir
  sehen Ihrer positiven Antwort mit Interesse
  entgegen
  if we get a favourable reply wenn die
  Antwort positiv ausfällt
favourite Lieblings-
  our favourite method die von uns bevorzugte
  Methode
fax: **by fax** per Telebrief
feature (*of product*) ein besonderes Merkmal
  one of the main features of ... eine der
  Haupteigenschaften von ...
February Februar
fee die Gebühr
feedback das Feedback
  if you give us more feedback wenn wir mehr
  Feedback von Ihnen bekommen
feel: **I feel certain/tired** ich bin sicher/müde
  I feel like ... ich habe Lust auf ...
felt-tip ein Filzstift
Fernschreiben telex
fernschriftlich by telex
Fernsprecher telephone
ferry die Fähre
fetch: **will you come and fetch me?** kommen
  Sie mich abholen?
Feuermelder fire alarm
few einige
  only a few nur ein paar
  a few days ein paar Tage
  fewer than ... weniger als ...

fiasco ein Fiasko
field das Gebiet
  in the field of ... auf dem Gebiet des/der ...
fieldwork Arbeit im Außendienst
fierce (*competition*) hart
fifty-fifty fifty-fifty
figure die Zahl
  let's look at the figures wir wollen die Zahlen
  ansehen
  the figures are quite clear die Zahlen sind
  ganz eindeutig
  sales figures die Verkaufsziffern
file die Akte
  (*box file etc*) der Ordner
  (*computers*) die Datei
  they're not on file sie sind nicht bei den
  Akten
Filiale branch
fill füllen
  to fill in a form ein Formular ausfüllen
film der Film
final letzte(r,s)
final demand die letzte Aufforderung
final offer das letzte Angebot
final draft der endgültige Entwurf
finalize fertigmachen
  we're still finalizing our plans wir sind noch
  bei der endgültigen Festlegung der Pläne
  another fortnight to finalize matters noch
  vierzehn Tage, um die Sache endgültig
  abzuschließen
finance finanzieren
  extra finance zusätzliche Finanzmittel
  to finance a project ein Projekt finanzieren
finance director der Finanzdirektor

ä [eh], au as in h*ow*, äu, eu [oy], ei as in I, ie [ee]
ö as in h*er*, ü, y as in h*u*ge, -b [-p], -d [-t], j [y], qu [kv]
    s- [z-], ß [ss], v [f], w [v], z [ts]

financial finanziell
the financial aspect der finanzielle Aspekt
financial assistance die finanzielle
Unterstützung
it makes financial sense es ist aus
finanzieller Sicht sinnvoll
the last financial year das letzte
Rechnungjahr
financially finanziell
financially sound finanziell gesichert
Finanzamt Inland Revenue
find finden
if you find it wenn Sie es finden
I've found a ... ich habe ein ... gefunden
fine gut, schön
50 marks fine eine Geldstrafe von fünfzig
Mark
Ok, that's fine das ist gut
finger der Finger
finish: I haven't finished ich bin noch nicht
fertig
well/poorly finished goods gut/schlecht
verarbeitete Waren
Finland Finnland
Finnish finnisch
fire: fire! Feuer!
he's been fired er ist entlassen worden
firm die Firma
a firm offer ein festes Angebot
a firm order eine definitive Bestellung
we need firmer control wir brauchen
strengere Kontrollen
firm up: we want to firm up on this order wir
wollen den Auftrag unter Dach und Fach
bringen
first erste(r,s)
I was first ich bin erster
at our first meeting bei unserer ersten
Besprechung

in the first place zunächst
at first zuerst
first class erster Klasse
first name der Vorname
fit: not fit for use unbrauchbar
    we'll fit a new part wir bringen ein neues Teil
    an
    it doesn't fit das paßt nicht
    can you fit us in tomorrow? können Sie uns
    morgen einen Termin geben?
fix (*date, meeting*) vereinbaren
    can you fix it? (*arrange, repair*) können Sie
    das machen?
fixed costs die Fixkosten
flat flach
    (*apartment*) eine Wohnung
flat rate eine Pauschale
flavour der Geschmack
flexible flexibel
flight number die Flugnummer
float (*the pound etc*) floaten
floor der Boden
    on the second floor im zweiten Stock
floppy disk die Diskette
flourishing gutgehend
flow: the flow of information der
    Informationsfluß
flowchart ein Flußdiagramm
flower die Blume
flu die Grippe
fluctuations Fluktuationen
fluent fließend
    he speaks fluent German er spricht fließend
    Deutsch
f.o.b. fob [fop], frei Schiff

ä [eh], au as in h*ow*, äu, eu [oy], ei as in I, ie [ee]
ö as in h*er*, ü, y as in h*u*ge, -b [-p], -d [-t], j [y], qu [kv]
s- [z-], ß [ss], v [f], w [v], z [ts]

....

foggy neblig
folder die Aktenmappe
follow folgen
   follow the instructions befolgen Sie die
   Anweisungen
   as follows wie folgt
   we'll follow it up wir gehen der Sache nach
   would you follow this up würden Sie der
   Sache bitte nachgehen
follow-up: what sort of follow-up are you
   planning? welche weiteren Maßnahmen
   planen Sie?
   follow-up publicity die Nachfaßwerbung
food das Essen
food poisoning die Lebensmittelvergiftung
foot der Fuß
» *1 foot=30.1 cm=0.3 metres*
f.o.r. frei Bahn
for für
   for 3 months drei Monate lang
   valid for 3 years drei Jahre gültig
   I'm for the idea ich bin für den Vorschlag
forbidden verboten
forecast: our production forecast die
   Prognose für unsere Produktion
   the forecast sales level die vorausgesagten
   Verkaufsziffern
foreign ausländisch
foreigner ein Ausländer
foreign exchange Devisen
foreign exchange market der Devisenmarkt
foresee vorhersehen
forget vergessen
   I forget, I've forgotten ich habe es vergessen
   don't forget vergessen Sie nicht
fork die Gabel
form (*document*) das Formular
formal formell
   (*person, matter*) förmlich

formal acceptance (*of invitation*) förmliche
   Zusage
   (*of goods*) formelle Annahme
format das Format
   in a new format in einem neuen Format
former: **the former** der/die/das erstere
formula die Formel
forthcoming (*visit etc*) bevorstehend
fortnight vierzehn Tage
fortunately zum Glück
forward vorwärts
   could you forward my mail? könnten Sie
   mir bitte die Post nachsenden?
forwarding address die Nachsendeadresse
forwarding agent der Spediteur
forwarding instructions die Lieferanweisungen
found (*company*) gründen
Fracht *freight*
Frachtbrief *bill of lading*
fragile zerbrechlich
framework (*for agreement*) der Rahmen
   within the framework of ... im Rahmen ...
France Frankreich
franchise die Franchise
frank: **I'll be frank** ich will ganz offen sein
franko *carriage paid*
fraud der Betrug
freak result ein außergewöhnliches Ergebnis
free frei
   admission free Eintritt frei
   when will he be free? wann hat er Zeit?
   one free in every twelve ordered ein
   Gratisexemplar pro zwölf bestellte
   free of charge kostenlos

ä [eh], au as in h*ow*, äu, eu [oy], ei as in I, ie [ee]
ö as in h*er*, ü, y as in h*u*ge, -b [-p], -d [-t], j [y], qu [kv]
   s- [z-], ß [ss], v [f], w [v], z [ts]

free port ein Freihafen
free sample eine Gratisprobe
freelance freiberuflich
freeze: a pay freeze ein Lohnstopp
frei ans Schiff free alongside ship
freight die Fracht
freight charges die Frachtkosten
freight collect per Nachnahme
frei Haus free house
frei Schiff free on board
frei Waggon free on rail
Fremdenzimmer rooms
French französisch
Frenchman Franzose
Frenchwoman Französin
frequent häufig
Friday Freitag
friend ein Bekannter/eine Bekannte
    (*more intimate*) ein Freund/eine Freundin
friendly freundlich
Frist period; deadline
from von
    from England aus England
    where is it from? woher kommt es?
    from the 14th June vom vierzehnten Juni an
    from then on von da an
    from £250 ab £250
front die Vorderseite
    in front of you vor Ihnen
    in the front vorn
    10% up front zehn Prozent im voraus
    how much up front cash? wieviel Geld im voraus?
fruitful (*talks*) fruchtbar
frustrating frustrierend
FS=Fernschreiben telex
fulfill (*conditions*) erfüllen
full voll
full-time (*work*) ganztags

function die Funktion
  (*verb*) funktionieren
fun: **it's fun** das macht Spaß
fundamental grundlegend
Fundbüro lost property
funny komisch
furniture Möbel
further weiter
  further information weitere Informationen
  for further details write to ... sollten Sie
  weitere Informationen wünschen, so schreiben
  Sie an ...
  further to your letter of ... mit Bezug auf Ihr
  Schreiben vom ...
future die Zukunft
  in future in Zukunft
futures Termingeschäfte
gadget eine Vorrichtung
gain: **a gain of 15%** ein Anstieg von fünfzehn
  Prozent
gallon die Gallone
» *1 gallon=4.55 litres*
gamble: **it's a gamble** es ist riskant
gap (*in market*) eine Marktlücke
garage (*repair*) eine Werkstatt
  (*petrol*) eine Tankstelle
  (*parking*) eine Garage
gas das Gas
  (*petrol*) das Benzin
gear der Gang
  (*equipment*) die Ausrüstung
Gebr.=Gebrüder Bros.
Gebühr fee; charges
Gefahr danger
Gegenverkehr oncoming traffic

ä [eh], au as in h*ow*, äu, eu [oy], ei as in I, ie [ee]
ö as in h*er*, ü, y as in h*u*ge, -b [-p], -d [-t], j [y], qu [kv]
s- [z-], ß [ss], v [f], w [v], z [ts]

Genehmigung *permit*
general allgemein
generally im allgemeinen
general manager der General Manager
generate (*demand*) erzeugen
generous großzügig
genius ein Genie
gentleman der Herr
gentlemen's agreement ein Gentlemen's
  Agreement
gents die Herrentoilette
genuine echt
geöffnet *open*
German deutsch
  the Germans die Deutschen
  (*person*) Deutscher/Deutsche
  I don't speak German ich spreche kein
  Deutsch
German Democratic Republic die Deutsche
  Demokratische Republik, die DDR [day-day-
  air]
» *TRAVEL TIP: see East Germany*
Germany Deutschland
ges., Gesamt- *total*
Geschäft *business; deal; shop*
Geschäftszeichen *reference*
Geschwindigkeitsbegrenzung *speed limit*
Gesellschaft *company*
gesture eine Geste
get: will you get me a...? holen Sie mir bitte
  ein ...?
  how do I get to ...? wie komme ich nach ...?
  where do I get off? wo muß ich aussteigen?
  where do you get your supplies? woher
  beziehen Sie Ihre Ware?
  you can't get them any cheaper Sie können
  sie nicht billiger bekommen
  where did you get it from? woher haben Sie
  das?

I'll get him to look at it ich sage ihm, er soll
es sich ansehen
we're not getting anywhere das bringt uns
nicht weiter
now we're getting somewhere jetzt kommen
wir der Sache schon näher
get back: **when can I get it back?** wann kann
ich es zurückbekommen?
when do we get back? wann sind wir zurück?
I'll get back to you ich werde noch auf Sie
zurückkommen
gilt-edged securities mündelsichere
Wertpapiere
gin Gin
gin and tonic ein Gin Tonic
girl ein Mädchen
Giro giro
giro: **postal giro** Postgiro
bank giro Bankgiro
giro cheque die Bankanweisung
Girokonto current account
give geben
I gave it to him ich habe es ihm gegeben
could you give us...? können Sie uns bitte ...
geben?
I'm practically giving it away das ist fast
geschenkt
glad froh
we were glad to hear that... wir haben uns
darüber gefreut, daß ...
glass das Glas
a glass of water ein Glas Wasser
glasses die Brille
Glatteis black ice
Gläubiger creditor

ä [eh], au as in h*o*w, äu, eu [oy], ei as in I, ie [ee]
ö as in h*e*r, ü, y as in h*u*ge, -b [-p], -d [-t], j [y], qu [kv]
s- [z-], ß [ss], v [f], w [v], z [ts]

....

Gleis *platform*

glue der Klebstoff

GmbH [gay-em-bay-hah] = ***Gesellschaft mit beschränkter Haftung*** *limited liability company; liability limited to extent of capital investment*

GmbH & Co. KG [gay-em-bay-hah oont koh kay-gay] *a partnership in which liability is borne by the partner which is a GmbH*

GNP das Bruttosozialprodukt

go gehen

where are you going? wo gehen Sie hin?

he's/it's gone er/es ist weg

when does the train go? wann fährt der Zug?

YOU MAY THEN HEAR ...

alle zehn Minuten *every ten minutes*

jede Stunde *every hour*

go against: that goes against our policy/ decision das ist gegen unsere Richtlinien/ unseren Beschluß

go ahead: we intend to go ahead with... wir wollen mit ... anfangen

go-ahead: if you give us the go-ahead wenn Sie uns Ihre Einwilligung geben

go along: I'll go along with that ich bin damit einverstanden

go back on: you're going back on what you said/what we agreed Sie weichen von unserer Vereinbarung ab

go down (*costs, sales*) zurückgehen

they're going down big in the UK sie sind ein großer Erfolg im Vereinigten Königreich

go for: we should be going for 20%/for growth wir sollten zwanzig Prozent/ Wachstum anstreben

go into: let's go into this in detail wir wollen uns mit dieser Sache eingehend befassen

go on: if things go on like this wenn alles so weitergeht

go over: I want to go over the results ich
  möchte die Ergebnisse durchsprechen
**go through: let's go through the figures/plans
  again** wir wollen die Zahlen/Pläne noch
  einmal durchgehen
go up (*prices*) steigen
goal (*objective*) das Ziel
gold das Gold
gold standard der Goldstandard, die
  Goldwährung
golf Golf
good gut
  their credit is good sie sind kreditwürdig
goodbye auf Wiedersehen
goods die Waren
goodwill (*of business*) der Goodwill
go-slow der Bummelstreik
government die Regierung
grace: period of grace die Respektfrist
grade (*of goods*) die (Güte)klasse
gradually allmählich
gramme ein Gramm
» *100 grammes=approx 3½ oz*
grant: government grants Staatszuschüsse
  we can grant an extension of ... wir können
  eine Verlängerung von ... gewähren
  to grant somebody credit jemandem Kredit
  gewähren
grateful dankbar
  I'm very grateful to you ich bin Ihnen sehr
  dankbar
gratitude die Dankbarkeit
great groß
  (*very good*) großartig
  great! Klasse!

ä [eh], au as in h*ow*, äu, eu [oy], ei as in I, ie [ee]
ö as in h*er*, ü, y as in h*u*ge, -b [-p], -d [-t], j [y], qu [kv]
  s- [z-], ß [ss], v [f], w [v], z [ts]

Greece Griechenland
greedy gierig
Greek griechisch
green grün
grey grau
grim (*outlook, meeting*) schlimm
gross brutto
Großhandel *wholesale*
Großhändler *wholesaler*
gross margin die Bruttospanne
gross profit der Bruttogewinn
ground: to help you get this off the ground
  um das in Gang zu bringen
  on the ground auf dem Boden
  on the ground floor im Erdgeschoß
grounds for complaint Grund zur Beschwerde
groundwork die Vorarbeit
group die Gruppe
grow wachsen
  a growing company ein wachsendes
  Unternehmen
growth das Wachstum
  a growth industry eine Wachstumsindustrie
guarantee die Garantie
  is there a guarantee? gibt es darauf
  Garantie?
  it's guaranteed for 2 years darauf sind zwei
  Jahre Garantie
  I can guarantee that das kann ich Ihnen
  garantieren
guaranteed loan die Garantieanleihe
guest der Gast
guess annehmen
  at a guess I'd say... schätzungsweise würde
  ich sagen, ...
  it's just a guess das ist nur geraten
guesstimate eine grobe Schätzung
guide der Führer
guidelines die Richtlinien

guilty schuldig
gültig valid
Gültigkeitsdauer period of validity
Güter goods
Gutschein voucher
Haben credit
haftbar liable
hair das Haar
  is there a hairdresser's here? gibt es hier einen Friseur?
» *TRAVEL TIP: hairdressers close on Mondays*
half halb
  in the first half of 1984 im ersten Halbjahr 1984
  at half price zum halben Preis
  half the size die halbe Größe
  half as much again noch einmal halb so viel
  one and a half anderthalb
half year das Halbjahr
half-yearly halbjährlich
hand die Hand
  it has been put in hand das wird gerade bearbeitet
  you've got everything to hand es steht Ihnen alles zur Verfügung
  the job's in safe hands die Sache ist in guten Händen
handbag die Handtasche
Handel trade
Handelskammer Chamber of Commerce
handkerchief ein Taschentuch
handle der Griff
  we can handle that das können wir machen
  who handled the order? wer hat den Auftrag bearbeitet?

ä [eh], au as in h*ow*, äu, eu [oy], ei as in I, ie [ee]
ö as in h*er*, ü, y as in h*u*ge, -b [-p], -d [-t], j [y], qu [kv]
s- [z-], ß [ss], v [f], w [v], z [ts]

handle with care Vorsicht – zerbrechlich!
handling charge die Bearbeitungsgebühr
damaged in handling beim Transport
beschädigt
Händler dealer
hand luggage das Handgepäck
handmade handgearbeitet
handy (*gadget*) praktisch
hangover der Kater
happen geschehen
  I don't know how it happened ich weiß
  nicht, wie es geschehen ist
  what's happening/happened? was ist los?
happy glücklich
  we would be happy to ... wir würden uns
  freuen, ...
  we're not happy with ... wir sind mit ... nicht
  zufrieden
hard hart
hardly kaum
hard sell aufdringliches Verkaufen, das Hard
  selling
hardware die Hardware
harm der Schaden
harmonious harmonisch
hate: I hate ... ich hasse ...
  I hate to have to tell you, but ... es ist mir
  unangenehm, Ihnen das sagen zu müssen,
  aber ...
Haupt- main
have haben
  I have ich habe
  he/she/it has er/sie/es hat
  you/we/they have Sie/wir/sie haben
  I/he/it had ich/er/sie/es hatte
  you/we/they had Sie/wir/sie hatten
  do you have ...? haben Sie ...?
  can I have some water/some more? kann
  ich etwas Wasser/noch etwas mehr haben?

I have to leave tomorrow ich muß morgen abreisen
when can you let us have it by? bis wann können wir es spätestens haben?
I'll have it sent ich werde es schicken lassen
to have something done etwas machen lassen
Hbf=Hauptbahnhof central station
he er
  he is er ist
head der Kopf
  the head of this department der Leiter dieser Abteilung
  the person heading up the team/the operation der Leiter des Teams/des Unternehmens
headache Kopfschmerzen
head office die Zentrale
headquarters die Zentrale
health die Gesundheit
  your health! zum Wohl!
hear hören
  we have heard that ... wir haben gehört, daß ...
  hear, hear (sehr) richtig!
heart attack ein Herzinfarkt
heat die Hitze
heated (*discussion*) hitzig
heating die Heizung
heavily (*in debt, overdrawn*) hoch (*committed*) schwer
heavy (*debts, expenses*) hoch (*commitments, workload*) schwer
hedge: as a hedge against inflation als Absicherung gegen die Inflation

---

ä [eh], au as in h*ow*, äu, eu [oy], ei as in I, ie [ee]
ö as in h*er*, ü, y as in h*u*ge, -b [-p], -d [-t], j [y], qu [kv]
s- [z-], ß [ss], v [f], w [v], z [ts]

heiß *hot*
hello hallo
help helfen
  can you help us? können Sie uns helfen?
  if you need any help falls Sie Hilfe brauchen
  help! Hilfe!
helpful (*person*) hilfsbereit
  (*talks*) nützlich
her sie
  will you give it to her? würden Sie es ihr bitte
  geben?
  it's her das ist sie
  it's her bag, it's hers es ist ihre Tasche, es ist
  ihre
here hier
  come here kommen Sie her!
Herren *gents*
Hersteller *manufacturer*
Herstellungskosten *manufacturing costs*
hesitate zögern
  please don't hesitate to get in touch bitte
  wenden Sie sich jederzeit an uns
hide verstecken
  no hidden extras keine versteckten Kosten
high hoch
  higher höher
  the highest offer das höchste Angebot
high-level (*talks*) auf hoher Ebene
high-powered (*executive, salesman*) sehr
  kompetent, Top-
him ihn
  will you give it to him? würden Sie es ihm
  geben?
  it's him das ist er
hindsight: with hindsight im nachhinein
hire *see* rent
hire purchase der Ratenkauf
his sein
  it's his idea das ist seine Idee

history: **the history of the deal** die
  Vorgeschichte des Geschäfts
hit: **we've been badly hit by ...** ... hat uns
  schwer getroffen
  it suddenly hit me es ist mir plötzlich
  aufgegangen
hitch: **there's been a slight hitch** es ist ein
  kleines Problem aufgetaucht
hive off (*department*) abspalten
HO [hah-oh] = *Handelsorganisation East
  German state retail shop*
Hochgarage multi-storey car park
Höchstgeschwindigkeit maximum speed
hold halten
hold up: **production has been held up** wir
  sind mit der Produktion in Verzug geraten
  sorry, I was held up ich wurde leider
  aufgehalten
hole das Loch
holiday der Urlaub
  Monday is a holiday Montag ist ein Feiertag
  we are closed for the summer holiday wir
  haben Betriebsferien
  I'll be on holiday ich bin im Urlaub
  see **public**
Holland Holland
home: **at home** zu Hause
  my home address meine Heimatanschrift
  the home market der Binnenmarkt
  home sales der Verkauf im Inland
  when we get home wenn wir zurückkommen
honest(ly) ehrlich
honour (*bill*) einlösen
  (*check*) begleichen
  (*commitments*) einhalten

ä [eh], au as in h*ow*, äu, eu [oy], ei as in I, ie [ee]
ö as in h*er*, ü, y as in h*uge*, -b [-p], -d [-t], j [y], qu [kv]
s- [z-], ß [ss], v [f], w [v], z [ts]

....

hope hoffen
  I hope that ... ich hoffe, daß ...
  I hope so/I hope not hoffentlich/hoffentlich
  nicht!
hospital das Krankenhaus
hospitality: thank you for your hospitality
  vielen Dank für Ihre Gastfreundschaft
host der Gastgeber
hostess die Gastgeberin
hot heiß
  they're selling like hot cakes sie gehen weg
  wie warme Semmeln
hotel das Hotel
  at my hotel in meinem Hotel
hour die Stunde
hourly (*rate*) Stunden-
house das Haus
how wie
  how many wie viele
  how much wieviel
  how often wie oft
  how long wie lang
  **how long have you been with this
  company?** wie lange sind Sie schon bei dieser
  Firma?
  how are you? wie geht es Ihnen?
however jedoch
  however much we try wie sehr wir uns auch
  bemühen
hundredweight
» *1 cwt=50.8 kilos or approx 'ein Zentner'; in
  Germany 'ein Zentner'=50 kilos; but in Austria
  and Switzerland 'ein Zentner'=100 kilos*
Hungarian ungarisch
Hungary Ungarn
hungry hungrig
  I'm hungry/not hungry ich habe Hunger/ich
  habe keinen Hunger
hurry: I'm in a hurry ich habe es eilig

please hurry! bitte beeilen Sie sich
there's no hurry es eilt nicht
if you can hurry things along wenn Sie die
Sache beschleunigen können
hurt: it hurts es tut weh
husband: my husband mein Mann
hypermarket ein Großmarkt
Hypothek mortgage
I ich
  I am ich bin
i.A.=im Auftrag on behalf of
ice das Eis
  with lots of ice mit viel Eis
ice-cream ein Eis
idea die Idee
  good idea eine gute Idee
  new ideas neue Ideen
  this will give you some idea of ... so
bekommen Sie eine Vorstellung von ...
ideal ideal
identical identisch
idiot der Idiot
if wenn, falls
  if not wenn nicht
ill krank
  I feel ill ich fühle mich nicht wohl
illegal illegal
illegible unleserlich
image das Image
  our company image das Image unserer
Firma
Imbiß(stube) snack bar
immediate unmittelbar
  in the immediate future in unmittelbarer
Zukunft

ä [eh], au as in h*ow*, äu, eu [oy], ei as in I, ie [ee]
ö as in h*er*, ü, y as in h*u*ge, -b [-p], -d [-t], j [y], qu [kv]
s- [z-], ß [ss], v [f], w [v], z [ts]

immediately sofort
Immobilien real estate; property
imperfect fehlerhaft
import der Import
important wichtig
   it's very important es ist sehr wichtig
import duty der Einfuhrzoll
importer der Importeur
import-export business das Import-Export-
   Geschäft
import licence die Importlizenz
import permit die Einfuhrerlaubnis
import restrictions die Einfuhr-
   beschränkungen
impossible unmöglich
impressive beeindruckend
improve verbessern
   an improved offer ein verbessertes Angebot
improvement die Verbesserung
   we've made some improvements wir haben
   einige Verbesserungen vorgenommen
in in
   in German auf deutsch
inch der Zoll
» *1 inch=2.54 cm*
incidental expenses die Nebenkosten
include einschließen
   does that include breakfast? ist Frühstück
   inbegriffen?
   that's all included alles inbegriffen
inclusive inklusive
income das Einkommen
incompetent unfähig
inconvenient unpassend
incorrect falsch
increase die Zunahme
   the increase in sales die Absatzsteigerung
   in order to increase the turnover um den
   Umsatz zu steigern

sales are increasing der Absatz steigt an
  at an increasing rate immer schneller
incredible unglaublich
incur (*costs, expenses*) machen
independent unabhängig
in-depth Tiefen-
India Indien
indication das Anzeichen
  as an indication of ... als Anzeichen für ...
indigestion die Magenverstimmung
indoors drinnen
industrial industriell, Gewerbe-
industrial action der Streik
industrial estate das Industriegebiet
industrial relations Arbeitsbeziehungen
industry die Industrie
inexpensive preisgünstig
inferior (*quality*) minderwertig
inflation die Inflation
influence der Einfluß
inform informieren
  **I am pleased to be able to inform you
  that ...** ich freue mich, Ihnen mitteilen zu
  können, daß ...
  please inform us when ... bitte teilen Sie uns
  mit, wann ...
  keep me informed halten Sie mich auf dem
  laufenden
  we'll keep you informed wir halten Sie auf
  dem laufenden
  you are very well informed Sie sind sehr gut
  informiert
informal (*meeting*) ungezwungen
  (*agreement*) informell
  (*dress*) zwanglos

ä [eh], au as in h*ow*, äu, eu [oy], ei as in I, ie [ee]
ö as in h*er*, ü, y as in h*u*ge, -b [-p], -d [-t], j [y], qu [kv]
s- [z-], ß [ss], v [f], w [v], z [ts]

....

information die Informationen
  do you have any information in English about ...? haben Sie Informationsmaterial auf englisch über ...?
  for your information zu Ihrer Kenntnisnahme
Inh., Inhaber owner; *(of passport etc)* holder
initial erste(r,s)
  to initial an agreement ein Abkommen paraphieren
injured verletzt
innocent unschuldig
input der Input
inside innen
  inside information Insider-Informationen
insist: I insist (on it) ich bestehe darauf
inspect kontrollieren
inspection die Inspektion
  regular inspections regelmäßige Kontrollen
  closer inspection showed that ... bei genauerer Prüfung hat sich gezeigt, daß ...
inspector der Inspektor
installations die Anlagen
instead statt dessen
  instead of ... an Stelle von ...
instruction die Anleitung
  as per your instructions laut Ihren Anweisungen
  instructions for use die Gebrauchs- anweisung
insurance die Versicherung
insurance company die Versicherungs- gesellschaft
insurance cover die Versicherungsdeckung
insurance policy die Versicherungspolice
insure versichern
insured versichert
  adequately insured against ... ausreichend gegen ...versichert

insurmountable unüberwindlich
intelligent intelligent
intend: we intend to ... wir beabsichtigen,
 ... zu ...
  what do you intend to do? was haben Sie
  vor?
intention die Absicht
  it was our intention to ... es war unsere
  Absicht, ... zu ...
Interbank die Interbank
interest das Interesse
  in the interests of speed der Schnelligkeit
  halber
  15% interest fünfzehn Prozent Zinsen
  interest rates Zinssätze
  we are very interested in ... wir interessieren
  uns sehr für ...
  are you interested in the idea? haben Sie
  Interesse an dieser Idee?
interesting interessant
  we find it very interesting wir halten es für
  sehr interessant
internal (*problems*) (betriebs)intern
international international
interpret: would you interpret for us?
  könnten Sie für uns dolmetschen?
interpreter der Dolmetscher/die Dolmetscherin
interruption die Unterbrechung
interview das Interview
  (*for job*) das Vorstellungsgespräch
into in
introduce: can I introduce ...? darf ich ...
  vorstellen?
invalid (*licence etc*) ungültig
invention die Erfindung

ä [eh], au as in h*ow*, äu, eu [oy], ei as in I, ie [ee]
ö as in h*er*, ü, y as in h*u*ge, -b [-p], -d [-t], j [y], qu [kv]
s- [z-], ß [ss], v [f], w [v], z [ts]

Inventur *stock-taking*
invest investieren
investment die Investition
investigate: we'll investigate the matter wir
   werden die Angelegenheit untersuchen
**investigations: our investigations have
   shown that ...** unsere Nachforschungen haben
   ergeben, daß ...
invisible unsichtbar
invitation die Einladung
   thank you for the invitation vielen Dank für
   Ihre Einladung
   invitation to tender eine Ausschreibung
invite: can I invite you out tonight? darf ich
   Sie für heute abend einladen?
invoice die Rechnung
   as per invoice laut Rechnung
   against invoice gegen Rechnung
   within 30 days of invoice innerhalb dreißig
   Tage nach Rechnungsdatum
   we'll invoice you direct wir schicken Ihnen
   die Rechnung direkt zu
   the amount invoiced der Rechnungsbetrag
   invoicing instructions Rechnungs-
   anweisungen
involve: what does it involve? was ist damit
   verbunden?
   it would involve extra costs das würde
   zusätzliche Kosten bedeuten
   we don't want to get involved in that wir
   möchten damit nichts zu tun haben
i.R.=im Ruhestand retd.
Ireland Irland
Irish irisch
   (*person*) Ire/Irin
iron: will you iron these for me? können Sie
   das bitte für mich bügeln?
iron out (*difficulties*) ausbügeln, ausgleichen
isolated: an isolated case ein Sonderfall

issue (*of shares*) die Ausgabe
it es
   it is es ist
Italian italienisch
Italy Italien
item der Posten
   all the items listed alle aufgeführten Posten
itemize: would you itemize it for me? könnten
   Sie es für mich postenmäßig aufschlüsseln?
   an itemized invoice eine postenmäßig
   aufgestellte Rechnung
jacket die Jacke
   (*of man's suit*) das Jackett
Jahresabschluß annual accounts
January Januar
Japan Japan
Japanese japanisch
   the Japanese die Japaner
jealous neidisch
jeopardize gefährden
jet der Jet
   private jet der Privatjet
jingle (*advertising*) der Werbespruch
jinx: the project is jinxed das Projekt ist
   verhext
job (*work*) die Arbeit
   (*order*) der Auftrag
   (*position*) die Stelle
   (*duty*) die Aufgabe
   just the job genau das richtige
   the job is yours Sie haben die Stelle/den
   Auftrag
   it's a big job es ist eine große Sache
   do you want the job? möchten Sie die Stelle/
   den Auftrag?

ä [eh], au as in h*o*w, äu, eu [oy], ei as in I, ie [ee]
ö as in h*e*r, ü, y as in h*u*ge, -b [-p], -d [-t], j [y], qu [kv]
s- [z-], ß [ss], v [f], w [v], z [ts]

you've done a very good job Sie haben sehr
gute Arbeit geleistet
what's your job? was sind Sie von Beruf?
to offer somebody a job jemandem eine
Stelle anbieten
that's your job das ist Ihre Aufgabe
it's your job to get that done das müssen Sie
erledigen
job description eine Stellenbeschreibung
job lot: we'll take them as a job lot wir
nehmen sie als (Waren)posten
job-satisfaction die berufliche Befriedigung
joint gemeinsam
joint venture das Joint-venture
joke der Witz
you must be joking das kann ja wohl nicht
Ihr Ernst sein
journey die Reise
have a good journey gute Reise!
judge: judging by... nach ... zu urteilen
July Juli
jump: a sudden jump in sales eine plötzliche
Absatzsteigerung
we mustn't jump to conclusions wir dürfen
keine vorschnellen Schlüsse ziehen
June Juni
junk der Ramsch
just: just two nur zwei
just a little nur ein bißchen
just there genau dort
that's just right das ist genau richtig
not just now jetzt nicht
just now gerade jetzt
he was here just now er war gerade hier
justifiable berechtigt
justifiably berechtigterweise
justify: how can you justify that? wie können
Sie das rechtfertigen?
kalt cold

Kapital *capital*
Kasse *cash desk*
Kauf *purchase*
Käufer *buyer*
Kaufmann *businessman*
keel: the business is on an even keel bei der Firma ist alles im Lot
keen begeistert
  I'm not keen ich bin nicht wild darauf
keep: can I keep it? darf ich es behalten?
  you keep it behalten Sie es
  keep the change stimmt so
  you didn't keep your promise Sie haben sich nicht an Ihr Versprechen gehalten
  it keeps on breaking down es geht immer wieder kaputt
  we'll keep on trying wir werden es weiterhin versuchen
kein Zutritt (für Unbefugte) *no admission (for unauthorized persons)*
key der Schlüssel
  the key facts die Schlüsselfakten
  a key person eine Schlüsselperson
  he plays a key role er spielt eine Schlüsselrolle
KG [kah-gay]=**Kommanditgesellschaft** *partnership; at least one partner fully liable and other(s) liable to extent of capital investment*
KGaA [kah-gay-ah-ah]=**Kommanditgesellschaft auf Aktien** *limited company in which at least one person has full liability and full powers; others liable to extent of their investment; as with AG there must be at least five founding directors*

ä [eh], au as in h*ow*, äu, eu [oy], ei as in I, ie [ee]
ö as in h*er*, ü, y as in h*u*ge, -b [-p], -d [-t], j [y], qu [kv]
s- [z-], ß [ss], v [f], w [v], z [ts]

killing: to make a killing einen Riesengewinn machen

kilo ein Kilo

» *conversion* : $\frac{kilos}{5} \times 11 = pounds$

kilos	1	1½	5	6	7	8	9
pounds	2.2	3.3	11	13.2	15.4	17.6	19.8

kilometre ein Kilometer

» *conversion* : $\frac{kilometres}{8} \times 5 = miles$

kilometres	1	5	10	20	50	100
miles	0.62	3.11	6.2	12.4	31	62

kind: that's very kind of you das ist sehr nett von Ihnen

would you be so kind as to... würden Sie so freundlich sein und ...

if you would kindly send us... wenn Sie so nett wären und uns ... schicken würden

Kinder *children*

knife das Messer

knockdown: at a knockdown price zu einem Schleuderpreis

know wissen

(*be acquainted with*) kennen

I don't know ich weiß nicht

I know him ich kenne ihn

please let us know bitte geben Sie uns Bescheid

please let us know what you decide bitte teilen Sie uns Ihre Entscheidung mit

I'll let you know ich gebe Ihnen Bescheid

know-how das Know-how

Konkurrenz *competition*

Konkurs *bankruptcy*

Konnossement *bill of lading*

Kontoauszug *statement*

Kontonummer *account number*

Kosten *costs*

Kostenvoranschlag *estimate; quote*

Krankenhaus hospital
Kredit credit; loan
Kreditbedingungen credit terms
Kto.=Konto a/c
Kunde client
Kurs exchange rate
label das Etikett
labour die Arbeit
labour costs die Arbeitskosten
labour-intensive arbeitsintensiv
labour-saving arbeitssparend
lack: there's a lack of ... es mangelt an ...
Ladeschein bill of lading
ladies die Damentoilette
Ladung loading; consignment
lady die Dame
Lager warehouse
lager ein helles Bier
Lagerbestand stock
land (*plane*) landen
langsam fahren drive slowly
language die Sprache
large groß
  by and large im großen and ganzen
last letzte(r,s)
  last year/week letztes Jahr/letzte Woche
  last night gestern abend
  at last! endlich!
  how long will this arrangement last? wie
  lange wird diese Vereinbarung dauern?
late: sorry I'm late entschuldigen Sie, daß ich
  zu spät komme
  it's a bit late es ist ein bißchen spät
  please hurry, I'm late bitte beeilen Sie sich,
  ich bin spät dran

ä [eh], au as in h*ow*, äu, eu [oy], ei as in I, ie [ee]
ö as in h*er*, ü, y as in h*u*ge, -b [-p], -d [-t], j [y], qu [kv]
    s- [z-], ß [ss], v [f], w [v], z [ts]

....

later später
   I'll come back later ich komme später zurück
   see you later! bis später
   at the latest spätestens
   the latest development die neueste
   Entwicklung
latter: the latter der/die/das letztere
laugh lachen
laughable lachhaft
launch: we are launching our new model wir
   bringen unser neues Modell auf den Markt
laundrette der Waschsalon
  » *TRAVEL TIP: not very many of these in*
   Germany; try a 'Sofortreinigung' (dry cleaner's)
lavatory die Toilette
law das Gesetz
lawyer der Rechtsanwalt
laxative ein Abführmittel
layout (*of premises*) die Anlage
   (*of report*) das Layout
lazy faul
lease mieten
   (*land, business premises*) pachten
   (*equipment*) leasen
   (*noun*) die Pacht
leasing agent die Leasinggesellschaft
least: not in the least nicht im geringsten
   at least mindestens
leather das Leder
leave: we're leaving tomorrow wir fahren
   morgen ab
   when does the plane leave? wann fliegt die
   Maschine ab?
   I left two shirts in my room ich habe zwei
   Hemden in meinem Zimmer liegenlassen
   can I leave this here? kann ich das
   hierlassen?
   I'll leave that up to you das überlasse ich
   Ihnen

....

let's leave that till later warten wir damit bis
später
Lebensgefahr danger
left: on the left links
left luggage (office) die Gepäckaufbewahrung
leg das Bein
legal legal
    legal aid die Rechtshilfe
    we intend to take legal action wir wollen
    gerichtlich vorgehen
    legal costs die Rechtskosten
    our legal advisor unser Rechtsberater
leisure: at your leisure wenn Sie Zeit haben
less weniger
    less the costs of ... abzüglich der Kosten für ...
let: let us help können wir helfen?
    will you let me off here? würden Sie mich
    bitte hier aussteigen lassen?
    let's go gehen wir
    when can you let us have them? wann
    können wir sie haben?
    we can't let that happen das dürfen wir nicht
    zulassen
letter der Brief; (*business letter*) das Schreiben
    are there any letters for me? habe ich Post?
    see pages 94–95
letterbox der Briefkasten
» *TRAVEL TIP: letterboxes in West Germany,
East Germany, Austria and Switzerland are
yellow*
letter of credit der Kreditbrief, das Akkreditiv
level: that will be decided at a higher level
    das wird von oben entschieden
    the level of profits die Gewinnlage
    the level of returns der Stand der Einkünfte

ä [eh], au as in h*ow*, äu, eu [oy], ei as in I, ie [ee]
ö as in h*er*, ü, y as in h*u*ge, -b [-p], -d [-t], j [y], qu [kv]
s- [z-], ß [ss], v [f], w [v], z [ts]

....

Steiner Kisten GmbH
z.Hd. Herrn Brüggemann
Bahnhofstraße 67
6500 Mainz 12

Ihr Zeichen	Ihre Nachricht vom	Unser Zeichen	Datum
B/mh	15.7.1983	MP/ks	1.8.1983

<u>Betr.:</u> 250 Holzkisten, Best. Nr. 06/4021

Sehr geehrter Herr Brüggemann,

wir nehmen Bezug auf Ihr Schreiben vom
15.7.1983 und teilen Ihnen mit, daß wir die am
30.6.1983 von Ihnen bestellten Holzkisten leider
nicht mehr rechtzeitig liefern können. Da
während der Betriebsferien vom 19.8. bis 14.9.
die Arbeit ganz eingestellt wird, wäre der
frühestmögliche Liefertermin der 29.9.1983.
Sollten Sie mit diesem Termin einverstanden
sein, so möchten wir Sie bitten, uns umgehend
Bescheid zu geben.

Als Anlage senden wir Ihnen den gewünschten
Prospekt, dem Sie alle Kistengrößen entnehmen
können, die wir herstellen.

Mit freundlichen Grüßen

Michael Peters
Verkaufsleiter

<u>Anlage</u>

....

Steiner Kisten GmbH
attn. Mr. Brüggemann
Bahnhofstraße 67
6500 Mainz 12

your ref	your letter of	our ref	date
B/mh	15.7.83	MP/ks	1.8.83

Re: 250 wooden boxes, order No. 06/4021

Dear Mr. Brüggemann,

We refer to your letter of 15.7.83 and regret to
have to inform you that we are no longer able to
deliver the wooden cases that you ordered from
us on 30.6.83 by the agreed date. Since
production here will close down completely from
August 19th to September 14th due to the factory
holidays, the earliest possible delivery date
would be 29.9.83. Please let us know
immediately if this date is acceptable to you.

Enclosed we are sending you the brochure that
you asked for. In this you will find all the box
sizes that we produce.

Yours sincerely,

Michael Peters
Sales Manager

Encl:

....

liabilities die Verbindlichkeiten
liability: we accept no liability for that wir
  übernehmen dafür keine Haftung
liable (*responsible*) haftbar
liaise: please liaise with Mr McGregor bitte
  betrachten Sie Herrn McGregor als Ihren
  Verbindungsmann
liaison die Verbindung
licence die Lizenz
  under licence unter Lizenz
licensing agreement das Lizenzabkommen
lid der Deckel
lie (*falsehood*) die Lüge
  he's lying er lügt
Lieferanweisungen delivery instructions
Liefertermin delivery date
Lieferung delivery
life das Leben
life assurance die Lebensversicherung
lift: do you want a lift? kann ich Sie
  mitnehmen?
  could you give me a lift? könnten Sie mich
  bitte mitnehmen?
  the lift isn't working der Fahrstuhl ist außer
  Betrieb
light das Licht
  (*not heavy*) leicht
  the lights aren't working das Licht geht
  nicht
  (*car*) die Scheinwerfer funktionieren nicht
  have you got a light? haben Sie Feuer?
like: would you like ...? möchten Sie ...?
  I'd like a .../I'd like to ... ich hätte gern .../ich
  möchte gern ...
  I like it das gefällt mir
  I don't like it das gefällt mir nicht
  like this one wie diese/dieser/dieses
  what's it like? wie ist es?
  do it like this machen Sie es so

limit: up to a certain limit bis zu einer gewissen
  Grenze
  a limited number of ... eine begrenzte Anzahl
  von ...
limited company eine Gesellschaft mit
  beschränkter Haftung, eine GmbH [gay-em-
  bay-hah]
line (*of business*) eine Branche
  (*of products*) das Warensortiment
  a new line in ... eine neue Sorte von ...
link die Verbindung
liqueur der Likör
list die Liste
listen zuhören
  listen! hören Sie zu!
list price der Listenpreis
literature (*brochures etc*) das Informationsmaterial
litre der Liter
» *1 litre=1¾ pints=0.22 gals*
little klein
  a little ice/a little more ein wenig Eis/noch
  etwas
  just a little nur ein bißchen
live leben
  I live in ... ich wohne in ...
  where do you live? wo wohnen Sie?
Lkw [el-kah-vay]=*Lastkraftwagen lorry*
load: each load jede Ladung
  they will be loaded next Tuesday sie
  werden nächsten Dienstag verladen
loan das Darlehen, der Kredit
local: could we try a local wine? könnten wir
  vielleicht einen Wein aus der Gegend
  probieren?

ä [eh], au as in h*o*w, äu, eu [oy], ei as in I, ie [ee]
ö as in h*e*r, ü, y as in h*u*ge, -b [-p], -d [-t], j [y], qu [kv]
s- [z-], ß [ss], v [f], w [v], z [ts]

a local restaurant ein Restaurant im Ort
a local call ein Ortsgespräch
a local firm eine Firma am Ort
we use local labour wir haben Arbeitskräfte
aus der Gegend
is it made locally? wird es hier hergestellt?
lock: the lock's broken das Schloß ist kaputt
I've locked myself out ich habe mich
ausgeschlossen
lonely einsam
long lang
I'd like to stay longer ich würde gern etwas
länger bleiben
that was long ago das ist lange her
how long? wie lange?
there's a long way to go yet da liegt noch viel
Arbeit vor uns
long-term langfristig
in the long term auf lange Sicht
look: can I have a look? darf ich mal sehen?
how do things look? wie sieht's aus?
I'm looking for ... ich suche ...
I'm just looking ich möchte mich nur
umsehen
let's look at the report wir wollen uns den
Bericht ansehen
look at that sehen Sie sich das an
look out! Vorsicht!
the figures look good die Zahlen sehen
vielversprechend aus
I look forward to hearing from you ich
freue mich, von Ihnen zu hören
I look forward to our next meeting ich sehe
unserem nächsten Zusammentreffen mit
Interesse entgegen
loose (*goods*) lose
lorry der Last(kraft)wagen, der Lkw [el-kah-
vay]
lorry-driver der Lkw-Fahrer

lose verlieren
    I've lost my ... ich habe mein ... verloren
    excuse me, I'm lost entschuldigen Sie bitte,
    ich habe mich verlaufen
    (*driving*) ich habe mich verfahren
    we're losing money wir verlieren dabei Geld
    nobody loses out keiner kommt zu kurz
loss der Verlust
    we made a loss wir haben mit Verlust
    gearbeitet
    at a loss mit Verlust
loss leader ein Lockvogelangebot
loss-making: it's a loss-making concern das
    ist eine Firma, die mit Verlust arbeitet
lost property (*office*) das Fundbüro
lot: a lot/not a lot viel/nicht viel
    a lot of people/wine viele Leute/viel Wein
    lots (of) jede Menge
    a lot more expensive sehr viel teurer
loud laut
lovely schön
low niedrig
    sales are at an all-time low der Absatz ist so
    niedrig wie noch nie
low-key (*approach, presentation*) zurückhaltend,
    unaufdringlich
loyal loyal
loyalty die Loyalität
lt. = *laut according to, as per*
luck Glück
    bad luck Pech
    good luck viel Glück!
lucky Glücks-
    you're lucky Sie haben Glück
    that's lucky das ist Glück

ä [eh], au as in h*ow*, äu, eu [oy], ei as in I, ie [ee]
ö as in h*er*, ü, y as in h*u*ge, -b [-p], -d [-t], j [y], qu [kv]
s- [z-], ß [ss], v [f], w [v], z [ts]

....

luggage das Gepäck
lump sum der Pauschalbetrag
lunch das Mittagessen
Luxembourg Luxemburg
luxury der Luxus
machine die Maschine
mad verrückt
madam gnädige Frau
magazine die Zeitschrift
magnificent großartig
Mahnung reminder
mail die Post
  is there any mail for me? habe ich Post?
mailing list die Adressenliste
mail order der Versand
mailshot die Massenpostsendung
main: the main problem das Hauptproblem
mainly hauptsächlich
main road die Hauptstraße
maintenance contract der Wartungsvertrag
major (company, new product) wichtig
  this is a major opportunity das ist *die* Gelegenheit
  the major points die Hauptpunkte
majority die Mehrheit
majority holding die Mehrheitsbeteiligung
make machen
  will we make it in time? schaffen wir das rechtzeitig?
  what is it made of? woraus ist es hergestellt?
  it's made of ... es ist aus ...
  it's not making money das bringt nichts ein
  I'll try to make him reconsider ich werde zusehen, daß er die Angelegenheit noch einmal überdenkt
man der Mann
management das Management
  it's a question of good management das ist eine Frage guten Managements

management problems die
Managementprobleme
our management are not in favour of unser
Management ist nicht für ...
manager der Manager
**production manager/sales manager/
publicity manager** der Produktionsleiter/
Verkaufsleiter/Publicitymanager
can I see the manager? kann ich den
Geschäftsführer sprechen?
manageress (*shop, restaurant*) die
Geschäftsführerin
managing director der leitende Direktor
Managerkrankheit *executive stress*
man-hour eine Mannstunde
Manko *deficit*
man-management die Personalführung
manpower die Arbeitskräfte
manual (*book*) das Handbuch
manufacture die Herstellung
manufacturer der Hersteller
manufacturing costs die Herstellungskosten
many viele
map die Landkarte
a map of ... eine Karte von ...
March März
margin (*in costing*) die Spanne
marginal (*improvement, difference*) geringfügig
mark: there's a mark on it es ist beschädigt
(*stained*) da ist ein Fleck drauf
Marke *brand*
market der Markt
on the market auf dem Markt
we're not in the market for ... wir sind nicht
an ... interessiert

ä [eh], au as in h*ow*, äu, eu [oy], ei as in I, ie [ee]
ö as in h*er*, ü, y as in h*uge*, -b [-p], -d [-t], j [y], qu [kv]
s- [z-], ß [ss], v [f], w [v], z [ts]

to bring something onto the market etwas auf den Markt bringen
what the market needs was der Markt braucht
we're looking for new markets wir suchen neue Absatzmärkte
there's no market for them es gibt dafür keinen Markt
the Money Market der Geldmarkt
to market something etwas vermarkten
it was badly marketed es wurde schlecht angeboten
it depends how you market it es hängt davon ab, wie Sie es anbieten
marketing das Marketing
I'm in marketing ich bin im Marketing tätig
our marketing policy unsere Marketing-Politik
we're very strong on marketing Marketing ist unsere starke Seite
marketing director der Marketing-Direktor
marketing manager der Marketing-Manager
market leader der Marktführer
market place: in the market place auf dem Markt
market research die Marktforschung
market trends die Markttendenzen
mark-up der Aufschlag
a 30% mark-up ein Aufschlag von dreißig Prozent
married verheiratet
marvellous wunderbar
mass-production die Massenproduktion
match: a box of matches eine Schachtel Streichhölzer
material das Material
matter: it doesn't matter das macht nichts
maturity (of bill) die Fälligkeit
maximize maximieren

maximum maximal
  (*noun*) das Maximum
  that's our maximum offer das ist unser
  höchstes Angebot
May Mai
may: may I ...? darf ich bitte ...?
  may I have ...? darf ich bitte ... haben?
maybe vielleicht
me mich
  with/from me mit/von mir
  will you send it to me? schicken Sie es bitte
  an mich
  it was me das war ich
meal das Essen
mean: what does this mean? was heißt das?
  what do you mean? was wollen Sie damit
  sagen?
  I mean it! ich meine es ernst
meantime: in the meantime in der
  Zwischenzeit
meet treffen
  we'll come to meet you wir holen Sie ab
  I've never met him ich habe ihn nie
  kennengelernt
meeting die Besprechung
  (*conference*) die Konferenz
  at our last meeting bei unserer letzten
  Besprechung
  I think we need another meeting ich glaube,
  wir müssen noch eine Besprechung ansetzen
Mehrwertsteuer value-added tax, VAT
member das Mitglied
memo die Aktennotiz
mend: can you mend this? können Sie das
  wieder in Ordnung bringen?

ä [eh], au as in how, äu, eu [oy], ei as in I, ie [ee]
ö as in her, ü, y as in huge, -b [-p], -d [-t], j [y], qu [kv]
s- [z-], ß [ss], v [f], w [v], z [ts]

mention: don't mention it gern geschehen
  as I mentioned in my letter wie bereits in
  meinem Schreiben erwähnt
menu die Speisekarte
  can I have the menu, please? die
  Speisekarte, bitte!; *see pages 106–109*
merchandise die Ware
merchandising das Merchandising
merger die Fusion
mess ein Durcheinander
message: are there any messages for me? hat
  jemand eine Nachricht für mich hinterlassen?
  can I leave a message for ...? kann ich eine
  Nachricht für ... hinterlassen?
Messe fair
metal das Metall
method die Methode
metre der Meter
» *1 metre=39.37 ins=1.09 yds*
microchip das Mikrochip
microcomputer der Mikrocomputer
mid: by mid June bis Mitte Juni
middle die Mitte
  by the middle of next month bis Mitte
  nächsten Monats
  in the middle in der Mitte
  the Middle East der Nahe Osten
middleman der Mittelsmann
middle management das mittlere Management
midnight Mitternacht
might: I might be wrong vielleicht hab' ich
  unrecht
  he might have gone er ist vielleicht schon
  gegangen
mile die Meile
» *conversion* : $\dfrac{miles}{5} \times 8 = kilometres$

miles	$\frac{1}{2}$	1	3	5	10	50	100
kilometres	0.8	1.6	4.8	8	16	80	160

milk die Milch
millimetre der Millimeter
mind: **I've changed my mind** ich habe es mir
anders überlegt
please bear this in mind vergessen Sie das
bitte nicht
my mind is made up ich habe mich schon
entschieden
I don't mind das macht mir nichts aus
do you mind if I ...? macht es Ihnen etwas
aus, wenn ich ...?
I'm sure they won't mind ich bin sicher, daß
sie nichts dagegen haben
never mind macht nichts
mine mein
mineral water ein Mineralwasser
minimize auf ein Minimum reduzieren
minimum das Minimum
minor (*problems*) kleiner
minus minus
minute die Minute
he'll be here in a minute er kommt gleich
just a minute einen Moment bitte
minutes das Protokoll
misgivings: **I have misgivings** ich habe
Bedenken
Miss das Fräulein
miss: **there's a ... missing** da fehlt ein ...
if we miss the deadline wenn wir die Frist
nicht einhalten (können)
I don't want to miss my plane ich möchte
meine Maschine nicht verpassen
mistake der Fehler
I think you've made a mistake ich glaube,
Sie haben sich geirrt

ä [eh], au as in h*ow*, äu, eu [oy], ei as in I, ie [ee]
ö as in h*er*, ü, y as in h*u*ge, -b [-p], -d [-t], j [y], qu [kv]
s- [z-], ß [ss], v [f], w [v], z [ts]

Vorspeisen	**Hors d'oeuvre**
Kaviar	*caviar*
Königinpastetchen	*chicken vol-au-vent*
Russische Eier	*egg mayonnaise*
Gänseleber-Pastete	*goose liver paté*
Heringssalat	*herring salad*
Austern	*oysters*
Krabbencocktail	*prawn cocktail*
geräucherter Aal	*smoked eel*
geräucherter Lachs	*smoked salmon*
Weinbergschnecken	*snails*

Suppen	**Soups**
Hühnerbrühe	*chicken broth*
Spargelcremesuppe	*cream of asparagus*
Gulaschsuppe	*goulash soup*
Linsensuppe	*lentil soup*
Ochsenschwanzsuppe	*oxtail soup*
Schildkrötensuppe	*real turtle soup*
Tomatensuppe	*tomato soup*

Salate	**Salads**
Selleriesalat	*celery salad*
Gurkensalat	*cucumber salad*
Endiviensalat	*endive salad*
Kopfsalat	*lettuce*
Rohkostplatte	*salad plate*
Wurstsalat	*sausage salad*
Tomatensalat	*tomato salad*

Vom Rind	**Beef**
Rinderlende	*beef tenderloin*
Rinderfillet	*fillet steak*
Sauerbraten	*marinaded potroast*
Bouletten (*Berlin*)	*meat balls*
Deutsches Beefsteak	*mince patty*
Rinderbraten	*pot roast*
Rostbraten (*Swabia*)	*steak with onion*
Rouladen	*stuffed beef roll*

Vom Schwein	**Pork**
Leberkäse (*S Ger*)	*baked pork and beef loaf*
gekochter Schinken	*boiled ham*
Kotelett	*chop*
Kassler, geräuchert und gegart	*smoked and braised pork chop*
Eisbein	*knuckles of pork*
Schweineschnitzel	*pork fillet*
Jägerschnitzel	*pork with mushrooms*
Zigeunerschnitzel	*pork with peppers and relishes*
Schweinebraten	*roast pork*
Schweinerollbraten	*rolled roast of pork*
Rippchen	*spareribs*
Spanferkel	*suckling pig*
Vom Kalb	**Veal**
Kalbshaxe	*leg of veal*
Kalbsnierenbraten	*roast veal with kidney*
Wienerschnitzel	*veal in breadcrumbs*
gefüllte Kalbsbrust	*veal roll*
Wild	**Game**
Hasenkeule	*haunch of hare*
Rehkeule	*haunch of venison*
Wildschweinkeule	*haunch of wild boar*
Rehbraten	*roast venison*
Rehrücken	*saddle of venison*
Rehgoulasch	*venison goulash*
Wildschweinsteak	*wild boar steak*
Fisch	**Fish**
Karpfen	*carp*
Aal	*eel*
Makrele	*mackerel*
Hecht	*pike*
Heringstopf	*pickled herrings*
Scholle	*plaice*

Schillerlocken	*smoked haddock roll*
Bückling	*smoked red herring*
geräucherte Sprotten	*smoked sprats*
Seezunge	*sole*
Forelle Müllerin Art	*trout with butter and lemon (breaded)*

Geflügel	**Poultry**
Taube	*pigeon*
Entenbraten	*roast duck*
Gänsebraten	*roast goose*
Hähnchen	*spring chicken*
Truthahn/Pute	*turkey*

Wurstsorten	**Sausages**
Bratwurst	*grilled pork sausage*
Bockwurst	*large Frankfurter*
Katenleberwurst	*smoked liver sausage*
Wurstsülze	*sausage in aspic*
Aufschnitt	*sliced cold cuts*

Beilagen	**Side dishes**
Salzkartoffeln	*boiled potatoes*
Klöße/Knödel	*dumplings*
Pommes frites	*French fried potatoes*
Bratkartoffeln	*fried potatoes*
Spätzle	*homemade noodles*
Nudeln	*pasta*
Kartoffelbrei/Püree	*potato purée*
Reis	*rice*

Gemüse	**Vegetables**
Artischocken	*artichokes*
Spargel	*asparagus*
Rosenkohl	*Brussels sprouts*
Karotten/Möhren	*carrots*
Blumenkohl	*cauliflower*
Grüne Gurke	*cucumber*
Grüne Bohnen	*green beans*

Sauerkraut	*green cabbage, finely chopped and pickled*
Erbsen	*green peas*
Weißkraut	*green cabbage*
Champignons/Pilze	*mushrooms*
Rotkraut	*red cabbage*
Spinat	*spinach*
Tomaten	*tomatoes*

Zubereitung	**Preparation**
Fisch blau	*blue (boiled fish)*
gekocht	*boiled*
geschmort	*braised/stewed*
gebacken	*fried*
vom Rost/Grill	*grilled*
gebraten	*roast*
geräuchert	*smoked*
gefüllt	*stuffed*
paniert	*with breadcrumbs*
mit Sahne	*with cream*
mit Rahm	*with sour cream*

Nachspeisen	**Desserts**
gemischtes Eis mit Sahne	*assorted ice creams with whipped cream*
Rote Grütze (*N Ger*)	*fruit blancmange*
Obstsalat	*fruit salad*
Eisbecher	*knickerbocker glory*

Kuchen- und Torten- spezialitäten	**Cake Specialities**
Apfelstrudel	*apple strudel*
Schwarzwälder Kirschtorte	*Black Forest cherry gateau*
Käse-Sahne-Torte	*cream cheese cake*
Eissplittertorte	*ice chip cake*
Nuß-Sahne-Torte	*nut cream cake*
Erdbeertorte mit Schlagsahne	*strawberry cake with whipped cream*

....

misunderstand: **don't misunderstand me**
verstehen Sie mich nicht falsch
misunderstanding das Mißverständnis
mix die Mischung
   a good mix of products eine gute Mischung
   von Produkten
mix-up ein Durcheinander
mobile beweglich
model das Modell
modern modern
modernize modernisieren
modification eine Modifizierung
moment ein Moment
   at the moment momentan
Monday Montag
money das Geld
   I've lost my money ich habe mein Geld
   verloren
   no money kein Geld
» *In West Germany the unit of 'eine Mark' is*
  made up of 100 'Pfennige'. Denominations are:
  (pfennigs) 1Pf, 2, 5, 10, 50; (marks) DM1, 2, 5;
  (notes) DM10, 20, 50, 100, 500, 1,000.
» *In East Germany the unit of 'eine Mark'*
  (Ostmark) is made up of 100 'Pfennige'.
  Denominations are: (pfennigs) 1pfg, 5, 10, 20,
  50; (marks) M1, 2, 5, 10, 20; (notes) M5, 10, 20,
  50, 100.
» *In Austria the unit of 'ein Schilling' is made up*
  of 100 'Groschen'. Denominations are:
  (groschen) 10Gr, 50; (schillings) ÖS1, 5, 10, 20;
  (notes) Ö20, 50, 100, 1,000.
» *In Switzerland the unit of 'ein Franken' is made*
  up of 100 'Rappen'. Denominations are:
  (rappen) 5Rp, 10, 20, 50, (francs) Fr1, 2, 5;
  (notes) Fr10, 20, 50, 100, 500, 1,000.
money order die Zahlungsanweisung
monitor (*results*) überwachen
monopoly das Monopol

month der Monat
monthly monatlich
more mehr
  can I have some more? kann ich noch etwas
  haben?
  more wine, please noch ein bißchen Wein,
  bitte
  no more nicht mehr
  more comfortable bequemer
  more than mehr als
morning der Morgen
  this morning heute morgen
  good morning guten Morgen
  in the morning am Morgenbeit
most: I like it most das gefällt mir am besten
  most of the time meistens
  most of the people die meisten Leute
motivated motiviert
motor der Motor
motorway die Autobahn
move: could you move your car? könnten Sie
  bitte Ihren Wagen wegfahren?
  he's moved to another department/
  company er hat die Abteilung/Firma
  gewechselt
  he's the man to get things moving das ist
  der Mann, der die Sache in Gang bringt
Mr Herr
Mrs Frau
Ms Frau
much viel
  much better/much more viel besser/viel
  mehr
  not much nicht viel
multinational ein multinationaler Konzern

ä [eh], au as in h*ow*, äu, eu [oy], ei as in I, ie [ee]
ö as in h*er*, ü, y as in h*u*ge, -b [-p], -d [-t], j [y], qu [kv]
s- [z-], ß [ss], v [f], w [v], z [ts]

must: I must have ... ich muß ... haben
I must not eat ... ich darf kein ... essen
you must do it Sie müssen es tun
you must not ... Sie dürfen nicht ...
that's a must das ist ein Muß
Muster sample
mutual: in our mutual interests in unserem
gegenseitigen Interesse
to our mutual satisfaction zu unserer beider
Zufriedenheit
to our mutual advantage zu unserem
beiderseitigen Vorteil
MwSt=Mehrwertsteuer value-added tax, VAT
Nachbestellung repeat order
Nachfrage demand
Nachlaß discount
name der Name
my name is ... mein Name ist ...
what's your (his/her) name? wie ist Ihr (sein/
ihr) Name?
napkin die Serviette
narrow eng
national national
nationality die Nationalität
nationalize verstaatlichen
natural natürlich
near: is it near? ist es in der Nähe?
near here in der Nähe
do you go near ...? kommen Sie in die Nähe
von ...?
where's the nearest ...? wo ist der/die/das
nächste ...?
nearly fast
neat (*drink*) pur
Nebenkosten incidental expenses
necessary nötig
as necessary bei Bedarf
it's not necessary das ist nicht nötig
necessitate erfordern

necessity die Notwendigkeit
need: I need a ... ich brauche ein ...
  we need more time wir brauchen mehr Zeit
  the need for ... der Bedarf an ...
negative negativ
  a negative response eine Absage, ein
  negativer Bescheid
negligent nachlässig
negotiable übertragbar
  not negotiable nicht übertragbar
negotiate: to negotiate a settlement eine
  Vereinbarung aushandeln
  we are currently negotiating with ... wir
  verhandeln zur Zeit mit ...
negotiations die Verhandlungen
negotiator der Unterhändler
neither: neither of them keiner von beiden
  neither ... nor ... weder ... noch
  neither do I ich auch nicht
nervous nervös
net netto
  net price der Nettopreis
  £5000 net £5.000 netto
  net of tax nach Steuerabzug
  the net profit margin die Reingewinnspanne
***netto** net*
network (*of distributors etc*) das Netz
never niemals
new neu
  I'm new to the job ich bin neu in dieser Stelle
news (*press*) die Nachrichten
  what news do you have about
  developments in ...? welche Neuigkeiten gibt
  es über Entwicklungen in ...?
newspaper die Zeitung

ä [eh], au as in h*ow*, äu, eu [oy], ei as in I, ie [ee]
ö as in h*er*, ü, y as in h*u*ge, -b [-p], -d [-t], j [y], qu [kv]
s- [z-], ß [ss], v [f], w [v], z [ts]

newspaper article der Zeitungsartikel
do you have any English newspapers?
haben Sie englische Zeitungen?
in the newspaper in der Zeitung
New Zealand Neuseeland
next der/die/das nächste
please stop at the next corner halten Sie
bitte an der nächsten Ecke
see you next month bis nächsten Monat
on my next trip auf meiner nächsten Reise
at the next opportunity bei der nächsten
Gelegenheit
next we have to ... als nächstes müssen wir ...
next to me neben mir
nice schön
nicht berühren do not touch
nicht öffnen do not open
Nichtraucher no smoking
Niederlassung branch
night die Nacht
good night gute Nacht
at night nachts
where's a good night club? wo gibt es einen
guten Nachtklub?
night-life das Nachtleben
night-porter der Nachtportier
no nein
no improvement keine Verbesserung
no change keine Änderung
no sales keine Verkäufe
no extra costs keine zusätzlichen Kosten
no way! auf keinen Fall!
No. Nr.
nobody niemand
nobody is buying them keiner kauft sie
noisy laut
my room's too noisy in meinem Zimmer ist
es zu laut
non- nicht-

non-committal zurückhaltend
  he was very non-committal er wollte sich
  überhaupt nicht festlegen
non-delivery die Nichtlieferung
non-dutiable nicht zollpflichtig
non-fulfilment die Nichterfüllung
non-productive unproduktiv
non-starter (*idea etc*) der Blindgänger
none: none of them keiner von ihnen
nonsense der Quatsch
normal normal
  when things are back to normal wenn alles
  wieder seinen gewohnten Gang geht
normally normalerweise
north der Norden
Northern Ireland Nordirland
Norway Norwegen
Norwegian norwegisch
not nicht
  I'm not hungry ich habe keinen Hunger
  not that one das nicht
  not me ich nicht
  I don't understand ich verstehe das nicht
  he didn't tell me er hat mir das nicht gesagt
notary der Notar
Notarzt emergency doctor
Notausgang emergency exit
note (*bank note*) der (Geld)schein
  I'll make a note of it ich schreibe mir das auf
  my notes of the meeting meine
  Konferenznotizen
  we note your ... wir nehmen Ihr ... zur
  Kenntnis
  please note that ... bitte nehmen Sie zur
  Kenntnis, daß ...

ä [eh], au as in h*ow*, äu, eu [oy], ei as in I, ie [ee]
ö as in h*er*, ü, y as in h*u*ge, -b [-p], -d [-t], j [y], qu [kv]
s- [z-], ß [ss], v [f], w [v], z [ts]

nothing nichts
notice (*on notice-board*) der Anschlag
   until further notice bis auf weiteres
   it has come to our notice that ... wir haben
   bemerkt, daß ...
   **we should like to bring the following to
   your notice** bitte nehmen Sie folgendes zur
   Kenntnis
   we need more notice than 3 weeks wir
   brauchen länger als drei Wochen vorher
   Bescheid
   how much advance notice do you need?
   wie lang im voraus müssen wir Ihnen Bescheid
   geben?
   not just like that without any notice das
   geht nicht so ohne Ankündigung
   I have handed in my notice ich habe
   gekündigt
   I didn't notice that das habe ich nicht
   bemerkt
notify: we will notify you when ... wir
   benachrichtigen Sie, wenn ...
   please notify us bitte benachrichtigen Sie uns
notorious berüchtigt
November November
now jetzt
nowhere nirgends
Nr.=Nummer No.
nuisance: it's a nuisance das ist ärgerlich
null and void null und nichtig
number (*figure*) die Zahl
   a number of problems einige Probleme
   number 57 Nummer siebenundfünfzig
   which number? welche Nummer?
object das Objekt
   do you object? haben Sie etwas dagegen?
   I object to that ich habe etwas dagegen
objection der Einwand
   I've no objections ich habe nichts dagegen

would you have any objections if ...? hätten
Sie etwas dagegen, wenn ...?
objective das Ziel
   (*adjective*) objektiv
obligation: without obligation unverbindlich
obligatory obligatorisch
**obliged: we would be very much obliged if
   you ...** wir wären Ihnen sehr dankbar, wenn
   Sie ...
obliging zuvorkommend
oblique: 2 oblique 4 zwei Schrägstrich vier
obsolescence das Veralten
obsolete veraltet
obstacle ein Hindernis
obtain (*get*) erhalten
obvious offensichtlich
obviously offensichtlich
   obviously not offensichtlich nicht
occasion: on the next occasion bei der
   nächsten Gelegenheit
   if the occasion should arise falls sich die
   Gelegenheit ergeben sollte
occasionally gelegentlich
occupation (*job*) der Beruf
   what's your occupation? was sind Sie von
   Beruf?
occupied beschäftigt
   is this seat occupied? ist dieser Platz noch
   frei?
occur vorkommen
o'clock *see* **time**
October Oktober
odd (*number*) ungerade
   (*strange*) seltsam
of von

ä [eh], au as in h*ow*, äu, eu [oy], ei as in I, ie [ee]
ö as in h*er*, ü, y as in h*u*ge, -b [-p], -d [-t], j [y], qu [kv]
s- [z-], ß [ss], v [f], w [v], z [ts]

off: 10% off zehn Prozent Ermäßigung
   at £3 off um £3 ermäßigt
   3% off for cash bei Barzahlung 3% Skonto
   the meeting is off die Besprechung fällt aus
   the deal is off die Sache ist nicht mehr
   diskutabel
offer das Angebot
   we accept your offer wir nehmen Ihr
   Angebot an
   I'll make you an offer ich mache Ihnen ein
   Angebot
   a special offer ein Sonderangebot
   what sort of conditions are you offering?
   wie sind Ihre Bedingungen?
   they only offered 10% sie haben nur zehn
   Prozent angeboten
office das Büro
official der Beamte
   the official version die offizielle Fassung
   in my official capacity in meiner offiziellen
   Funktion
off-load ausladen
Öffnungszeiten opening hours
often oft
OHG [oh-hah-gay]=*offene Handels-*
   gesellschaft general partnership with at least
   two founding partners; each is fully liable to the
   full extent of his personal assets
oil das Öl
OK okay
old alt
old-fashioned altmodisch
omit auslassen
on auf
   I haven't got it on me ich habe es nicht bei
   mir
   on Friday am Freitag
   on television im Fernsehen
   the deal is on again das Geschäft gilt wieder

OK, you're on okay, abgemacht
once einmal
    at once sofort
    once it is signed wenn es erst einmal
    unterschrieben ist
oncosts die Gemeinkosten
one ein
    (*number*) eins
    the red one der/die/das rote
one-off: a one-off job/order ein einmaliger
    Auftrag/einmaliges Angebot
    we'll do this one as a one-off wir behandeln
    das als eine einmalige Angelegenheit
only nur
    this is the only one das ist der/die/das einzige
open offen
    (*shop*) geöffnet
    when do you open? wann machen Sie auf?
    to open an account ein Konto eröffnen
    to open a new branch eine neue Zweigstelle
    eröffnen
    to open a letter of credit einen Kreditbrief
    eröffnen
open-ended offen
operate (*machine*) bedienen
    the area of business in which we operate
    der Geschäftsbereich, in dem wir tätig sind
operating capital das Betriebskapital
operating costs (*of a business*) die
    Betriebskosten
operation: our overseas operations unsere
    Transaktionen im Ausland
    when we put this new system into
    operation wenn wir dieses neue System in
    Kraft setzen

ä [eh], au as in h*o*w, äu, eu [oy], ei as in I, ie [ee]
ö as in h*er*, ü, y as in h*u*ge, -b [-p], -d [-t], j [y], qu [kv]
s- [z-], ß [ss], v [f], w [v], z [ts]

....

operator (*tel*) die Vermittlung
  (*of machine*) die Bedienungsperson
opinion die Meinung
  in our opinion unserer Meinung nach
  what's your opinion? wie ist Ihre Meinung
  dazu?
opportunity die Gelegenheit
  I was glad to have the opportunity of ... ich
  habe mich gefreut, daß ich die Gelegenheit
  hatte, ... zu ...
opposite: opposite the hotel gegenüber vom
  Hotel
option die Option
  if you'd like an option on the next model
  wenn Sie beim nächsten Modell gern die
  Option hätten
  we'll give you first option wir geben Ihnen
  das Vorkaufsrecht
  we have no option wir haben keine andere
  Wahl
optional: that's optional das ist Ihnen
  freigestellt
  optional extras Extrazubehör
or oder
orange (*colour*) orange
order der Auftrag
  if we place an order with you for ... falls wir
  Ihnen einen Auftrag über ... erteilen
  the last order hasn't arrived die letzte
  Lieferung ist nicht angekommen
  if we can win this order wenn wir diesen
  Auftrag bekommen können
  we have a very full order book wir sind
  auftragsmäßig voll ausgelastet
  there's not much in the order book wir
  haben eine schlechte Auftragslage
  the parts are still on order die Teile sind
  noch nicht angekommen
  in order to ... um ... zu ...

the goods we ordered die Waren, die wir
bestellt haben
could we order now? (*in restaurant*) können
wir jetzt bestellen?
thank you, we've already ordered danke,
wir haben bereits bestellt
order form das Bestellformular
order number die Bestellnummer
ordinary gewöhnlich
ordinary shares die Stammaktien
organization: good/poor organization gute/
schlechte Organisation
organize organisieren
origin: country of origin das Herkunftsland
original Original-
the original das Original
originally ursprünglich
other: the other one der/die/das andere
do you have any others? haben Sie
irgendwelche anderen?
otherwise sonst
ought: it ought to be here by now das sollte
eigentlich inzwischen hier sein
ounce die Unze
» *1 ounce=28.35 grammes*
our unser
that's ours das gehört uns
out aus
that's 5% out das stimmt um fünf Prozent
nicht
9 out of 10 neun von zehn
is he still out? ist er immer noch weg?
outlet (*sales -*) die Verkaufsstelle
outline: the broad outlines (of the proposal)
die groben Umrisse (des Vorschlags)

ä [eh], au as in h*ow*, äu, eu [oy], ei as in I, ie [ee]
ö as in h*er*, ü, y as in h*u*ge, -b [-p], -d [-t], j [y], qu [kv]
s- [z-], ß [ss], v [f], w [v], z [ts]

output der Output
outside: **outside advisors** die Außenberater
outstanding (*invoice, payment*) ausstehend
   5000 is still outstanding 5.000 stehen noch
   aus
over: **over here/there** hier/dort drüben
   over 40 über vierzig
   it's all over es ist alles vorbei
   over a period of 6 months über einen
   Zeitraum von sechs Monaten
   over and above that darüber hinaus
overcome (*difficulties*) überwinden
overdraft die Kontoüberziehung
overdraft facility die Überziehungsmöglichkeit
overdrawn überzogen
overdue (*payment*) überfällig
overheads die laufenden Kosten
overnight (*stay, travel*) über Nacht
overseas Auslands-
oversleep verschlafen
   I overslept ich habe verschlafen
overstock zu hoch bestücken
overtime die Überstunden
owe: **what do we owe you?** was sind wir Ihnen
   schuldig?
   money owing to us die Außenstände
   owing to wegen
own: **my own car** mein eigenes Auto
   I'm on my own ich bin allein hier
owner der Eigentümer
pack eine Packung
package das Paket
packaging die Verpackung
packing (*act*) das Packen
   (*material*) die Verpackung
packing case die Kiste
   (*cardboard*) der Karton
packing instructions die Verpackungs-
   vorschriften

packing list die Packliste
page (*of book*) die Seite
  could you page him? können Sie ihn bitte
  ausrufen lassen?
pain der Schmerz
  I've got a pain in my ... mir tut mein ... weh
pain-killers schmerzstillende Mittel
pair das Paar
Pakistan Pakistan
pale blaß
pallet die Palette
paper das Papier
  (*newspaper*) die Zeitung
papers (*documents*) die Unterlagen
parcel das Paket
pardon (*didn't understand*) wie bitte?
  I beg your pardon (*sorry*) entschuldigen Sie
  bitte
parent company die Muttergesellschaft
park: where can I park? wo kann ich parken?
*Parken nur mit Parkscheibe parking discs
  required (attach to windscreen, indicates when
  parking began; can be bought at stationery
  shops, department stores and garages)*
Parken verboten no parking
Parkplatz car park
part der Teil
  (*of machine*) das Teil
  part-consignment die Teillieferung
  part-load die Teilladung
  part-owner der Miteigentümer
  part-payment die Teilzahlung
particular besondere
  in particular besonders
particulars die Einzelheiten

ä [eh], au as in h*ow*, äu, eu [oy], ei as in I, ie [ee]
ö as in h*er*, ü, y as in h*u*ge, -b [-p], -d [-t], j [y], qu [kv]
    s- [z-], ß [ss], v [f], w [v], z [ts]

partner der Teilhaber
partnership eine offene Handelsgesellschaft,
   eine OHG [oh-hah-gay]
party (*group*) die Gruppe
   (*celebration*) die Party
   (*to contract*) die Partei
   both parties are agreed that ... beide
   Parteien sind sich darin einig, daß ...
Passiva *liabilities*
pass on: I'll pass it on to him (*information*) das
   teile ich ihm mit
   (*report etc*) das gebe ich ihm
passport der Reisepaß
past: in the past in der Vergangenheit
patent das Patent
   we have applied for the patent wir haben
   das Patent angemeldet
patient: be patient! Geduld!
pattern (*on material*) das Muster
Pauschale *lump sum*
pay bezahlen
   how shall we pay you? wie sollen wir Sie
   bezahlen?
   to pay the money back das Geld
   zurückzahlen
   can I pay, please? ich möchte gerne zahlen
» *TRAVEL TIP: in bars, pubs etc it's usual to pay*
   when you're leaving and not when you order
payable zahlbar
payee der Zahlungsempfänger
payer der Zahler
payment die Zahlung
   payment will be made in 3 instalments die
   Zahlung erfolgt in drei Raten
   method of payment die Zahlungsart
   conditions of payment die Zahlungs-
   bedingungen
   monthly payments of ... Monatsraten in
   Höhe von ...

we are still awaiting payment of ... wir
erwarten noch Ihre Zahlung in Höhe von ...
peak (*of figures, production*) die Spitze
pedestrian crossing der Fußgängerüberweg
» *TRAVEL TIP: be warned, the Germans take the*
red light for pedestrians rather more seriously
than we do; on-the-spot fines can happen
pen der Kugelschreiber
have you got a pen? haben Sie etwas zum
Schreiben?
penalty clause die Strafklausel
pencil der Bleistift
pension die Pension
people die Leute
the German people die Deutschen
if people like the product wenn das Produkt
gut ankommt
people say ... man sagt, ...
per: per night/week/person pro Nacht/Woche/
Person
as per instructions laut Anweisung
as per contract laut Vertrag
per cent das Prozent
you get 5% Sie bekommen fünf Prozent
percentage der Prozentsatz
a fixed percentage ein fester Prozentsatz
your percentage is ... Ihr Anteil beträgt ...
Prozent
on a percentage basis auf prozentualer Basis
perfect perfekt
performance (*of machine, employee, company*)
die Leistung
perhaps vielleicht
period der Zeitraum
permanent dauernd

ä [eh], au as in h*ow*, äu, eu [oy], ei as in I, ie [ee]
ö as in h*er*, ü, y as in h*uge*, -b [-p], -d [-t], j [y], qu [kv]
s- [z-], ß [ss], v [f], w [v], z [ts]

permission die Erlaubnis
permit die Genehmigung
person die Person
  in person persönlich
personal(ly) persönlich
personnel das Personal
personnel department die Personalabteilung
personnel director der Personalchef
persuade: we want to persuade you to ... wir
  möchten Sie überreden, ... zu ...
petrol das Benzin
petrol station die Tankstelle
» *TRAVEL TIP: 'Super' is 4-star; 'Normal' or*
  'Benzin' correspond to both 3-star and 2-star
phase das Stadium, die Phase
phase in allmählich einführen
phase out auslaufen lassen
phone *see* **telephone**
photograph die Fotografie
pick up (*improve*) besser werden
picture das Bild
piece das Stück
  a piece of ... ein Stück ...
pin down: to pin somebody down jemanden
  festnageln
pink rosa
pint ein Pint
» *1 pint=0.57 litres*
pipe die Pfeife
  (*metal*) das Rohr
pipe tobacco der Pfeifentabak
pity: it's a pity das ist schade
Pkw [pay-kah-vay]=*Personenkraftwagen*
  (private) motor car
place der Platz
  (*town*) der Ort
  is this place taken? ist hier noch frei?
  the meeting will take place in London die
  Konferenz findet in London statt

to place an order with somebody jemandem
einen Auftrag erteilen
plain (*food*) (gut)bürgerlich
(*not patterned*) einfarbig
plan der Plan
  according to plan planmäßig
  plans of the building Pläne vom Gebäude
  we are planning to ... wir haben vor, ... zu ...
  it's still at the planning stage es ist noch in
  der Planung
  plan of action das Aktionsprogramm
plane das Flugzeug
plant (*factory*) das Werk
  (*equipment*) die Anlagen
plastic das Plastik
platform der Bahnsteig
  which platform please? welches Gleis, bitte?
pleasant angenehm
please: could you please ...? könnten Sie
  bitte ...?
  (yes) please ja, bitte
  pleased to meet you sehr angenehm
  pleased with ... mit ... zufrieden
pleasure das Vergnügen
  my pleasure gern geschehen
plenty: plenty of ... viel ...
plus plus
p.m. nachmittags
pocket die Tasche
point der Punkt
  there are three points es gibt drei Punkte
  that's a very important point das ist ein
  ganz wichtiger Punkt
  point 16 on the list Punkt Nummer sechzehn
  auf der Liste

ä [eh], au as in h*ow*, äu, eu [oy], ei as in I, ie [ee]
ö as in h*er*, ü, y as in h*u*ge, -b [-p], -d [-t], j [y], qu [kv]
    s- [z-], ß [ss], v [f], w [v], z [ts]

**we'd like to draw your attention to the
following points** wir möchten Sie auf die
folgenden Punkte aufmerksam machen
from our/ your point of view aus unserer/
Ihrer Sicht
four point six vier Komma sechs
could you point to it? können Sie bitte darauf
zeigen?
point of sale die Verkaufsstelle
at point of sale an der Verkaufsstelle
point of sale material das Werbematerial an
der Verkaufsstelle
Poland Polen
police die Polizei
get the police holen Sie die Polizei
» *TRAVEL TIP: dial 110*
policeman der Polizist
police station die Polizeiwache
policy (*of company*) die Politik
(*insurance*) die Police
Polish polnisch
polish (*for shoes*) die Schuhcreme
could you polish my shoes? könnten Sie
bitte meine Schuhe putzen?
polite höflich
politics die Politik
polluted verschmutzt
polythene bag die Plastiktüte
pool (*swimming*) das Schwimmbad
poor arm
poor quality schlechte Qualität
popular beliebt
a very popular line ein sehr beliebter Artikel
portable tragbar
porter der Portier
(*rail, airport*) der Gepäckträger
Porto carriage; postage
Portugal Portugal
Portuguese portugiesisch

position die Position
  I'm not in a position to comment ich bin
  nicht in der Lage, mich dazu zu äußern
positive positiv
  a positive response eine Zusage, ein positiver
  Bescheid
possession der Besitz
  the goods will be in your possession ... die
  Waren werden ... bei Ihnen sein
possibility die Möglichkeit
possible möglich
  could you possibly ...? könnten Sie
  eventuell ...?
  as ... as possible so ... wie möglich
post (*job*) die Stelle
  it'll be in the post tomorrow es wird morgen
  aufgegeben
  I'll have it posted to you ich lasse es Ihnen
  zuschicken
postage das Porto
postcard eine Postkarte
poster das Plakat
poste restante postlagernd
post office das Postamt
postpone verschieben (**until** auf)
postwendend by return of post
potential potentiell
  it has a lot of potential es ist sehr
  ausbaufähig
pound das Pfund
  » *conversion:* $\dfrac{pounds}{11} \times 5 = kilos$

pounds	1	3	5	6	7	8	9
kilos	0.45	1.4	2.3	2.7	3.2	3.6	4.1

  NB: a German Pfund=500 grammes

ä [eh], au as in h*ow*, äu, eu [oy], ei as in I, ie [ee]
ö as in h*er*, ü, y as in h*u*ge, -b [-p], -d [-t], j [y], qu [kv]
  s- [z-], ß [ss], v [f], w [v], z [ts]

practical praktisch
precedent der Präzedenzfall
prefer: **I prefer this one** das gefällt mir besser
  I'd prefer to ... ich würde lieber ...
  I'd prefer a ... ich hätte lieber ein ...
Preis price
premises die Räumlichkeiten
premium der Bonus
  (*insurance*) die Prämie [pray-mee-uh]
premium offer das Extraangebot
present: **at present** zur Zeit
presentation (*of new product*) die Präsentation
  (*of bill of exchange*) die Vorlage
presentation pack die Display-Packung, das
  Display
president der Präsident
Press: **the Press** die Presse
press: **could you press these?** könnten Sie die
  bitte bügeln?
pressure: **you must put more pressure on**
  them Sie müssen mehr Druck auf sie ausüben
  he's under a lot of pressure er steht unter
  großem Druck
pre-tax vor Besteuerung
pretty hübsch
  it's pretty good es ist ganz gut
previous früher
  at our previous meeting bei unserer
  früheren Besprechung
  the previous agreement die frühere
  Vereinbarung
  does he have any previous experience? hat
  er Berufserfahrung?
price der Preis
  your prices are very reasonable/high Ihre
  Preise sind recht angemessen/hoch
  we don't want to price ourselves out of the
  market wir wollen mit unseren Preisen doch
  konkurrenzfähig bleiben

price list die Preisliste
price range die Preisklasse
pricing policy die Preispolitik
pricing structure die Preisstruktur
principal (*of order etc*) der Auftraggeber
   (*of investment*) das Kapital
   (*of debt*) die Schuldsumme
print drucken
   we enclose a colour print of ... beiliegend
   senden wir Ihnen ein Farbfoto von ...
printed matter Drucksache
printout der Ausdruck
prior: I have a prior engagement ich habe
   schon einen Termin
priority die Priorität
   it's not a priority das ist nicht vorrangig
   in order of priority nach Dringlichkeit
   will you treat this as a priority? behandeln
   Sie das bitte vorrangig
private privat
   a private discussion ein persönliches
   Gespräch
   a private company eine Privatgesellschaft
privatize privatisieren
probably wahrscheinlich
   probably not wahrscheinlich nicht
problem das Problem
   no problem kein Problem
procedure das Verfahren
proceedings: we shall take proceedings
   against you/them wir werden gerichtlich
   gegen Sie/sie vorgehen
process der Prozeß
   it's being processed right now es wird jetzt
   gerade bearbeitet

ä [eh], au as in how, äu, eu [oy], ei as in I, ie [ee]
ö as in her, ü, y as in huge, -b [-p], -d [-t], j [y], qu [kv]
s- [z-], ß [ss], v [f], w [v], z [ts]

....

process engineering die Verfahrenstechnik
produce produzieren
product das Produkt
production die Produktion
  we start production ... wir beginnen ... mit
  der Produktion
production manager der Produktionsleiter
**professional : a very professional piece of
  work** eine sehr fachmännische Arbeit
  not a very professional approach keine
  sehr professionelle Methode
profit der Gewinn
profit margin die Gewinnspanne
profit and loss account die Gewinn- und
  Verlustrechnung
profitability die Rentabilität
profitable gewinnbringend
profit sharing die Gewinnbeteiligung
pro-forma invoice die Proformarechnung
program (*computers*) das Programm
programme (*plan*) der Plan
progress: we are making good progress wir
  machen gute Fortschritte
  what progress have you made? was für
  Fortschritte haben Sie gemacht?
progress report der Bericht
  we need a monthly progress report wir
  brauchen einen Monatsbericht über den Stand
  der Entwicklung
project das Projekt
promise: do you promise? versprechen Sie
  das?
  I promise ehrlich
promissory note der Schuldschein
promote (*product*) auf den Markt bringen
  (*employee*) befördern
  it's been well/badly promoted es wurde gut/
  schlecht beworben
promotion (*of product*) die Werbung

for promotion purposes für Werbezwecke
pronounce: how do you pronounce it? wie
spricht man das aus?
properly richtig
property das Eigentum
(*land*) Grundstücke
proposal der Vorschlag
protect schützen
proud stolz
we are proud of our record wir sind stolz auf
unsere Leistungen
prove: I can prove it ich kann es beweisen
provided, providing vorausgesetzt
provisional(ly) provisorisch
proviso der Vorbehalt
public: the public die Öffentlichkeit
to create more public awareness die
Öffentlichkeit sensibilisieren
to monitor the public's reaction die
Reaktion der Öffentlichkeit überwachen
public company eine Aktiengesellschaft,
eine AG [ah-gay]
to go public in eine Aktiengesellschaft
umgewandelt werden
public convenience eine öffentliche Toilette
» *TRAVEL TIP: there are not very many public
conveniences in Germany; try the railway
station; the attitude towards using cafe etc is
the same as in Britain*
public holiday gesetzlicher Feiertag
» *TRAVEL TIP: public holidays are:*
New Year's Day *Neujahr*
Good Friday *Karfreitag (not Austria)*
Easter Monday *Ostermontag (not GDR)*
May Day *Erster Mai*

ä [eh], au as in h*ow*, äu, eu [oy], ei as in I, ie [ee]
ö as in h*er*, ü, y as in h*uge*, -b [-p], -d [-t], j [y], qu [kv]
s- [z-], ß [ss], v [f], w [v], z [ts]

Ascension Day *Christi Himmelfahrt (not GDR)*
Whit Monday *Pfingstmontag*
National Unity Day *Tag der deutschen Einheit
(17th June) (West Germany only)*
All Saints' Day *Allerheiligen (1st Nov) (not
GDR)*
Day of Prayer and Repentance *Buß- und
Bettag (mid Nov) (West Germany only)*
Christmas Day *1. (erster) Weihnachtsfeiertag*
Boxing Day *2. (zweiter) Weihnachtsfeiertag; in
the mainly Catholic parts there is also:*
Epiphany *Heilige Drei Könige (not GDR)*
Corpus Christi *Fronleichnam (not GDR)*
Assumption *Mariä Himmelfahrt (not GDR)*
» *in the GDR also:* GDR National Day
Nationalfeiertag der DDR (7th Oct);
» *in Austria also:* Austrian National Holiday
Nationalfeiertag (26th Oct);
Immaculate Conception *Mariä Empfängnis
(8th Dec);*
» *in Switzerland also:* Swiss National Holiday
Bundesfeier (1st August)
publicity die Werbung
publicity brochure der Werbeprospekt
publicity budget der Werbeetat
publicity campaign die Werbekampagne
publicity manager der Publicitymanager
publicity material das Werbematerial
pull ziehen
punctual pünktlich
puncture eine Reifenpanne
purchase der Kauf
　(*verb*) kaufen
purchase order die Auftragsbestätigung
pure rein
purple violett
purpose der Zweck
　on purpose mit Absicht
purse das Portemonnaie

push drücken
  (*products on market*) puschen
  we want to push this line hard wir möchten
  diesen Artikel puschen
put: where can I put ...? wo kann ich ... hintun?
  we want to put the deadline back wir
  möchten die Frist verlängern
qualified: I'm not qualified to comment ich
  bin nicht kompetent, um einen Kommentar
  abzugeben
qualitative qualitativ
quality die Qualität
quality control die Qualitätskontrolle
quality control department die Abteilung für
  Qualitätskontrollen
quantify quantifizieren
quantitative quantitativ
**quantity: what sort of quantity do you
  envisage?** welche Menge stellen Sie sich vor?
quarter ein Viertel
  (*quarter year*) das Quartal
  a quarter of an hour eine Viertelstunde
quarterly vierteljährlich
question die Frage
  do you have any other questions? haben Sie
  sonst noch Fragen?
questionnaire der Fragebogen
queue die Schlange
quick schnell
  that was quick das ging schnell
quiet ruhig
  a quiet time of the year eine ruhige Zeit
quite ganz
  quite a lot ziemlich viel
  quite! genau

ä [eh], au as in how, äu, eu [oy], ei as in I, ie [ee]
ö as in her, ü, y as in huge, -b [-p], -d [-t], j [y], qu [kv]
s- [z-], ß [ss], v [f], w [v], z [ts]

....

Quittung *receipt*

quota (*of work*) das Pensum
(*of goods*) das Kontingent

quotation, quote der Kostenvoranschlag

quote: we'd like to quote for it wir möchten
Ihnen dafür einen Kostenvoranschlag geben
at the price we quoted zu dem von uns
angebotenen Preis

Rabatt *discount*

radio das Radio

rail: by rail per Bahn

rain der Regen
it's raining es regnet

raincoat der Regenmantel

raise (*finance*) aufbringen
(*rate*) erhöhen

range (*of products*) das Sortiment
a new range ein neues Sortiment

rare selten
(*steak*) blutig

rate: the rate of exchange der Wechselkurs
our rates for this year unsere Preise für
dieses Jahr
the current rate of increase/growth die
derzeitige Steigerungs-/Wachstumsrate
at a monthly rate of 2% bei einer Monatsrate
von zwei Prozent
at any rate auf jeden Fall

rather: I'd rather have a ... ich hätte lieber
ein ...
I'd rather not lieber nicht!
it's rather expensive es ist ganz schön teuer

Rauchen verboten *no smoking*

Raucher *smoking compartment*

raw materials die Rohstoffe

razor der Rasierapparat

razor blades Rasierklingen

rd.=rund *approx.*

reach (*agreement*) erreichen

read: **you read it** lesen Sie es bitte
something to read etwas zu lesen
ready: **when will it be ready?** wann ist es
fertig?
real (*genuine*) echt
the real cost der Effektivpreis
really wirklich
reason der Grund
there are several reasons why ... es gibt
verschiedene Gründe dafür, warum ...
reasonable vernünftig
receipt (*in restaurant etc*) die Quittung
can I have a receipt, please? kann ich bitte
eine Quittung haben?
we are in receipt of ... wir haben ... erhalten
please acknowledge receipt bitte bestätigen
Sie den Erhalt
on receipt of ... nach Erhalt ...
recently kürzlich
reception (*hotel, also welcome*) der Empfang
at reception am Empfang
receptionist der Empfangschef
(*lady*) die Empfangsdame
receive (*goods, order*) erhalten
recession die Rezession
Rechnung *invoice*
Rechnungsdatum *date of invoice*
Rechnungsjahr *financial year*
Rechnungsnummer *invoice number*
recognize (*person*) wiedererkennen
(*effort etc*) anerkennen
recommend: **can you recommend ...?** können
Sie ... empfehlen?
reconsider: **we are willing to reconsider** wir
sind bereit, es noch einmal zu überlegen

ä [eh], au as in h*ow*, äu, eu [oy], ei as in I, ie [ee]
ö as in h*er*, ü, y as in h*u*ge, -b [-p], -d [-t], j [y], qu [kv]
s- [z-], ß [ss], v [f], w [v], z [ts]

record (*adjective*) Rekord-
  in record time in Rekordzeit
  a record level ein Rekordstand
  this is strictly off the record nur unter uns
red rot
  in the red in den roten Zahlen
  out of the red aus den roten Zahlen
reduce (*price*) ermäßigen
  (*costs*) senken
reduction (*in price*) die Ermäßigung
  (*in costs*) die Senkung
refer: we refer to your recent letter of the ...
  wir nehmen Bezug auf Ihr letztes Schreiben
  vom ...
reference: with reference to ... mit Bezug
  auf ...
  our/your reference unser/Ihr Zeichen
reference number das Zeichen
refuse: I refuse ich weigere mich
  they are refusing to pay sie weigern sich zu
  zahlen
regard: with regard to ... in bezug auf ...
  regarding your inquiry bezüglich Ihrer
  Anfrage
  as regards price/quality was den Preis/die
  Qualität betrifft
  with kind regards Mit freundlichen Grüßen
region das Gebiet
  in this region in diesem Gebiet
  in the region of £5000 etwa £5.000
registered: I want to send it registered ich
  möchte es per Einschreiben schicken
regret: I very much regret that ... ich bedaure
  sehr, daß ...
  we regret to hear that ... wir hören mit
  Bedauern, daß ...
regular regelmäßig
regulations die Bestimmungen
Reisebüro travel agency

**relation: the relations between our two
companies** die Beziehungen zwischen
unseren beiden Firmen
in the interests of good relations im
Interesse guter Beziehungen
relationship das Verhältnis
relevant relevant
rely: you can rely on it Sie können sich darauf
verlassen
remaining: the remaining sums/work die
restlichen Beträge/restliche Arbeit
remember: don't you remember? wissen Sie
das nicht mehr?
I'll always remember das werde ich nie
vergessen
if I remember rightly wenn ich mich recht
daran erinnere
remind: we would remind you that ... wir
möchten Sie daran erinnern, daß ...
reminder die Mahnung
final reminder die letzte Mahnung
renew (*contract etc*) erneuern
rent: can I rent a car? kann ich ein Auto
mieten?
repair: can you repair it? können Sie es
reparieren?
repeat: could you repeat that? könnten Sie das
bitte wiederholen?
repeat order eine Nachbestellung
replace ersetzen
replacement parts Ersatzteile
reply die Antwort
(*to advert*) die Zuschrift
in reply to your letter in Beantwortung Ihres
Schreibens

ä [eh], au as in h*ow*, äu, eu [oy], ei as in I, ie [ee]
ö as in h*er*, ü, y as in h*u*ge, -b [-p], -d [-t], j [y], qu [kv]
s- [z-], ß [ss], v [f], w [v], z [ts]

report der Bericht
we shall report back to you wir werden
Ihnen Bericht erstatten
who does he report to? wer ist sein
Vorgesetzter?
representative der Vertreter
reputation der Ruf
request der Wunsch
on request auf Wunsch
**requirements: we hope this meets your
requirements** wir hoffen, daß das Ihren
Wünschen entspricht
our present stock requirements unsere
momentanen Bestandserfordernisse
rescue retten
research forschen
research and development Forschung und
Entwicklung
reservation die Reservierung
I want to make a reservation for ... (*hotel*)
ich möchte ein Zimmer für ... bestellen
(*theatre*) ich möchte einen Platz für ...
reservieren lassen
reserve: can I reserve a seat/table? kann ich
einen Platz/Tisch reservieren lassen?
YOU MAY THEN HEAR ...
wie war der Name, bitte? *what name, please?*
für wann, bitte? *for what time?*
we reserve the right to ... wir behalten uns
das Recht für ... vor
resign: he's resigned er ist zurückgetreten
responsibility: this is your responsibility Sie
tragen dafür die Verantwortung
we cannot accept responsibility wir können
keine Verantwortung übernehmen
responsible verantwortlich
rest der Rest
you keep the rest stimmt so
restaurant das Restaurant

Restbestrag *remaining balance*
result: as a result of this als Ergebnis davon
  this year's results die Ergebnisse dieses
  Jahres
  excellent results ausgezeichnete Ergebnisse
retailer der Einzelhändler
retail outlet das Einzelhandelsgeschäft
retail price der Einzelhandelspreis
retired pensioniert
return: a return (ticket) to ... eine
  Rückfahrkarte nach ...
  by return of post postwendend
  please reply by return of telex wir bitten um
  umgehende Rückantwort per Telex
  the returns on this investment die Gewinne
  aus der Investition ·
  return on capital der Kapitalertrag
  if the returns are satisfactory wenn die
  Einkünfte zufriedenstellend sind
  returns *(goods sent back)* die Retouren
  **we are returning the substandard
  specimens** wir senden die minderwertigen
  Exemplare zurück
reverse charge call ein R-Gespräch
» *TRAVEL TIP: reverse charge calls are not
  possible within Germany*
revise *(plan)* überarbeiten
rich reich; *(food)* schwer
ridiculous lächerlich
right: you don't have the right to ... Sie haben
  kein Recht, ... zu ...
  that's right das stimmt
  you're right Sie haben recht
  on the right rechts
  right here genau hier

ä [eh], au as in h*ow*, äu, eu [oy], ei as in I, ie [ee]
ö as in h*er*, ü, y as in h*u*ge, -b [-p], -d [-t], j [y], qu [kv]
s- [z-], ß [ss], v [f], w [v], z [ts]

. . . .

rights die Rechte
  we keep all the rights wir behalten alle
  Rechte
  if we grant you the manufacturing rights
  wenn wir Ihnen die Produktionslizenz
  gewähren
rights issue eine Aktienausgabe
rip off: **it's a rip-off** das ist Wucher
rise (*in prices, costs*) der Anstieg
  rising costs steigende Kosten
road die Straße
  which is the road to ...? wo geht es nach ...?
rob: **I've been robbed** ich bin bestohlen worden
room das Zimmer
  have you got a (single/double) room? haben
  Sie ein (Einzel/Doppel)zimmer frei?
  for one night/for three nights für eine
  Nacht/für drei Nächte
  YOU MAY THEN HEAR ...
  mit oder ohne Bad? *with or without bath?*
  für wieviele Nächte/Personen? *for how many*
  nights/people?
  tut mir leid, wir sind voll ausgebucht/wir
  haben nichts mehr frei *sorry, we're full*
room service der Zimmerservice
roughly ungefähr
round: **in round figures** rund
  to round a figure up eine Zahl aufrunden
  it's my round das ist meine Runde
route die Strecke
  please specify delivery route bitte geben Sie
  den genauen Versandweg an
  by the usual sea route auf dem normalen
  Seeweg
royalties Tantiemen
rubber der Gummi
rubberband ein Gummiband
rubbish Unsinn
rude unhöflich

Ruhetag closed all day
rum ein Rum
  rum and coke Cola mit Rum
run: a run on the market ein Ansturm auf den
  Markt
running costs (*for organization*) die
  Betriebskosten
Russia Rußland
Russian russisch
sad traurig
  we are sad to hear wir bedauern, daß ...
safe sicher
salary das Gehalt
Saldo balance
sale der Verkauf
sale: on a sale or return basis auf
  Verkaufsbasis mit Rückgaberecht
  they're not for sale sie sind unverkäuflich
sales der Absatz, der Umsatz
  sales are improving/dropping off der
  Absatz steigt/geht zurück
  volume of sales das Verkaufsvolumen
  total sales for the past year der
  Gesamtverkauf des Vorjahres
sales campaign die Verkaufskampagne
sales department die Verkaufsabteilung
sales director der Verkaufsdirektor
sales drive die Verkaufskampagne
salesman der Verkäufer
  he is a good salesman er ist ein guter
  Verkäufer
sales manager der Salesmanager, der
  Verkaufsleiter
**sales-orientated: a more sales-orientated
  approach** eine verkaufsorientiertere Methode

ä [eh], au as in h*ow*, äu, eu [oy], ei as in I, ie [ee]
ö as in h*er*, ü, y as in h*u*ge, -b [-p], -d [-t], j [y], qu [kv]
s- [z-], ß [ss], v [f], w [v], z [ts]

sales outlet die Verkaufsstelle
sales person der Verkäufer/die Verkäuferin
sales target das Verkaufsziel
same der-/die-/dasselbe
  the same again please das gleiche noch mal
  bitte
  the same to you (danke) gleichfalls
sample ein Muster, ein Probeexemplar
  the sample models die Muster(proben)
  not up to sample nicht mustergetreu
satisfaction: to our/your complete
  satisfaction zu unserer/Ihrer vollsten
  Zufriedenheit
satisfactory zufriedenstellend
  a very satisfactory solution eine sehr
  zufriedenstellende Lösung
  your performance is not satisfactory Ihre
  Leistung ist nicht zufriedenstellend
  the standard of work is not satisfactory die
  Arbeit ist nicht zufriedenstellend
satisfy: we are not satisfied with ... wir sind
  mit ... nicht zufrieden
  I hope you will be satisfied with ... ich hoffe,
  Sie sind mit ... zufrieden
  we are not satisfied that everything
  possible has been done wir sind nicht davon
  überzeugt, daß alles mögliche getan wurde
Saturday Samstag
sauna die Sauna
save: this way we save £5000 auf diese Weise
  sparen wir £5.000
  it saves a lot of bother das erspart viel Mühe
  in order to save time um Zeit zu sparen
saving: a considerable saving in costs/time
  eine beträchtliche Kosten-/Zeitersparnis
say sagen
  how do you say ... in German? wie heißt ...
  auf deutsch?
  what did he say? was hat er gesagt?

what do you say to that? was sagen Sie dazu?
do we have a say in ...? haben wir bei ... ein
Mitspracherecht?
Schaden damage
schedule der Terminplan
   on/behind schedule (*travel*) pünktlich/
   verspätet
   work is on schedule die Arbeit verläuft
   programmgemäß
   work is behind schedule wir sind mit der
   Arbeit im Verzug
scheduled flight der Linienflug
Schlafwagen sleeper
Schließfächer luggage lockers
Schlußverkauf sale
schnaps ein Schnaps
» *some schnaps varieties are:*
   Anis *aniseed brandy;* **Brombeergeist**
   blackberry brandy; **Enzian** *gentian;* **Fenchel**
   fennel; **Genever** *juniper berries;*
   Himbeergeist *raspberry brandy;*
   Kirschgeist/Kirschwasser *cherry brandy;*
   Korn *grain;* **Kümmel** *caraway seed brandy;*
   Steinhäger *juniper berries;*
   Zwetschgenwasser *plum brandy*
   a 'Doppelkorn' or a 'Doppelkümmel' is stronger:
   38 Vol.% (or 76° in UK system); most varieties
   of schnaps, however, will have a minimum
   strength of 76°
Schreiben letter
Schuldner debtor
scissors: a pair of scissors eine Schere
scope (*of project etc*) der Umfang
   beyond the scope of these talks über den
   Rahmen dieser Gespräche hinaus

ä [eh], au as in h*o*w, äu, eu [oy], ei as in I, ie [ee]
ö as in h*e*r, ü, y as in h*u*ge, -b [-p], -d [-t], j [y], qu [kv]
s- [z-], ß [ss], v [f], w [v], z [ts]

....

Scot Schotte/Schottin
Scotland Schottland
Scottish schottisch
scratch der Kratzer
sea das Meer
  by sea auf dem Seeweg
sea freight die Seefracht
season die Saison
  in the high/low season in der Hochsaison/
  Nebensaison
seat der (Sitz)platz
  is this somebody's seat? ist hier noch frei?
seat belt der Sicherheitsgurt
second zweite(r,s)
  (*time*) die Sekunde
  just a second einen Moment, bitte
second class zweiter Klasse
second hand gebraucht
seconds (*goods*) zweite Wahl
secretary die Sekretärin
sector: in the private/public sector im
  privaten/öffentlichen Bereich
secure (*order*) erhalten
  (*loan*) (ab)sichern
security (*for loan, of premises etc*) die Sicherheit
see sehen
  oh, I see ach so!
  have you seen ...? haben Sie ... gesehen?
  can I see the samples? kann ich die Muster
  sehen?
  I'd like to see your figures ich möchte Ihre
  Zahlen sehen
seem scheinen
  it seems so es sieht so aus
Seeweg: auf dem Seeweg by sea
Selbstkostenpreis cost price
seldom selten
selection (*of goods*) die Auswahl
self-financing selbstfinanzierend

self-service Selbstbedienung
sell verkaufen
   to sell something to somebody jemandem
   etwas verkaufen
   if you can sell them the idea wenn Sie ihnen
   die Idee verkaufen können
   they are selling well/slowly sie verkaufen
   sich gut/langsam
send senden
   I'll send one to you ich sende Ihnen eins zu
   would you send us some samples? könnten
   Sie uns bitte einige Proben zuschicken?
   the goods are to be sent by container die
   Waren sollen per Container verschickt werden
   to send something by post/by telex etwas
   per Post/Telex senden
sender der Absender
separate getrennt
   under separate cover mit getrennter Post
   that's a separate matter das ist ganz was
   anderes
   it's a separate company das ist eine Firma
   für sich
September September
serial number die Seriennummer
series die Serie
   a new series eine neue Serie
serious (*situation*) ernst
   (*mistake, problem*) schwerwiegend
   I'm serious ich meine es ernst
   this is serious das ist ernst
   is it serious? ist es schlimm?
**service: we're not satisfied with the service
   we're getting** wir sind mit dem Service nicht
   zufrieden

ä [eh], au as in h*ow*, äu, eu [oy], ei as in I, ie [ee]
ö as in h*er*, ü, y as in h*u*ge, -b [-p], -d [-t], j [y], qu [kv]
s- [z-], ß [ss], v [f], w [v], z [ts]

we are pleased to be of service to you wir freuen uns, Ihnen behilflich sein zu können
his service to the company seine Verdienste in der Firma
it's all part of the service das gehört alles zum Service
service industries der Dienstleistungssektor
service station die Tankstelle
servicing contract der Wartungsvertrag
servicing manual die Wartungsanleitung
set: a set of new parts ein Satz neuer Teile
let's set a date wir wollen einen Termin festsetzen
let's set a new deadline wir wollen eine neue Frist festsetzen
to set up a company eine Firma gründen
settle: I want to settle this before I leave ich möchte das abschließen, bevor ich abreise
please settle your account bitte gleichen Sie Ihr Konto aus
please settle within 30 days bitte bezahlen Sie innerhalb von dreißig Tagen
settlement: a satisfactory settlement eine befriedigende Regelung
in settlement of our account zur Begleichung unserer Rechnung
we look forward to receiving your settlement wir erwarten Ihre Zahlung
settlement discount Skonto
several mehrere
shake schütteln
to shake hands die Hand schütteln
let's shake hands on it wir wollen es mit Handschlag bekräftigen
» *TRAVEL TIP: it is normal to shake hands each time you meet someone and when you leave someone*
shame: what a shame wie schade
shampoo ein Schampoo(n)

shandy ein Bier mit Limonade
  (*in South Germany*) eine Radlermaß
shape up: it's shaping up well es entwickelt
  sich gut
share (*in company*) die Aktie
  we must share the blame daran sind wir
  beide schuld
share capital das Aktienkapital
share-holder der Aktionär
sharp practice unsaubere Geschäfte
shave rasieren
shaver der Rasierapparat
shaving foam der Rasierschaum
she sie
  she is sie ist
sherry ein Sherry
ship das Schiff
  by ship per Schiff
  (*send*) versenden
  (*by sea also*) verschiffen
  they'll be shipped to you next week sie
  gehen nächste Woche an Sie ab
shipment: the next shipment of ... die nächste
  Sendung ...
  they will be ready for shipment on ... sie
  werden am ... zum Versand fertig sein
  each shipment jede Sendung
shipping agent die Reederei
shipping documents die Versandpapiere
shipping instructions die
  Versandanweisungen
shirt das Hemd
shock der Schock
shoe der Schuh
shop das Geschäft

ä [eh], au as in h*ow*, äu, eu [oy], ei as in I, ie [ee]
ö as in h*er*, ü, y as in h*u*ge, -b [-p], -d [-t], j [y], qu [kv]
  s- [z-], ß [ss], v [f], w [v], z [ts]

I've some shopping to do ich muß noch ein
paar Einkäufe machen
shop steward der Vertrauensmann
short kurz
   at short notice kurzfristig
   I'm three short ich habe drei zu wenig
short cut die Abkürzung
shortage die Knappheit
shortfall (*in figures, supplies*) das Defizit
short-term kurzfristig
   in the short term auf kurze Sicht
show: the items on show die ausgestellten
Artikel
   please show me bitte zeigen Sie mir
showcase der Schaukasten
shower: with shower mit Dusche
shrink-wrapped eingeschweißt
shut schließen
   when do you shut? wann machen Sie zu?
Sicherheit security
sick krank
side die Seite
   he does that on the side er macht das
nebenbei
   we're on your side wir sind auf Ihrer Seite
   side street die Seitenstraße
   by the side of the road am Straßenrand
sight: payable on sight zahlbar bei Sicht
   three days after sight drei Tage nach Sicht
   when we have sight of your order wenn uns
Ihr Auftrag vorliegt
sight bill der Sichtwechsel
sign (*notice*) ein Zeichen
   please sign here bitte hier unterschreiben
   to sign a contract einen Vertrag
unterzeichnen
   it's not signed es ist nicht unterschrieben
   I'm not signing that! das unterschreibe ich
nicht!

signature die Unterschrift
silly dumm
silver das Silber
similar ähnlich
simple einfach
since: since last week seit letzter Woche
   (*because*) weil
sincere aufrichtig
   yours sincerely Mit freundlichen Grüßen
   see **letter**
single: single room ein Einzelzimmer
   I'm single ich bin ledig
   a single/two singles to ... einmal einfach/
   zweimal einfach nach ...
sit: can I sit here? kann ich mich hierher
   setzen?
site: a good/bad site ein guter/schlechter Platz
situation die Situation
   the financial/economic situation die
   finanzielle/wirtschaftliche Lage
   in the present situation in der momentanen
   Situation
   a cut-back situation eine Rationalisierungs-
   situation
size die Größe
skill das Geschick
skilled worker ein gelernter Arbeiter
skirt der Rock
Skonto (*settlement*) discount
sleep: I can't sleep ich kann nicht schlafen
sleeper (*rail*) der Schlafwagen
sleeping pill eine Schlaftablette
slide (*phot*) das Dia
slide presentation eine Diavorführung
sliding scale eine gleitende Skala

ä [eh], au as in h*ow*, äu, eu [oy], ei as in I, ie [ee]
ö as in h*er*, ü, y as in h*u*ge, -b [-p], -d [-t], j [y], qu [kv]
   s- [z-], ß [ss], v [f], w [v], z [ts]

slow langsam
   that's too slow das ist zu langsam
   you're slowing down Sie werden langsamer
   could you speak a little slower? könnten Sie
   bitte etwas langsamer sprechen?
small klein
small change das Kleingeld
smoke der Rauch
   do you smoke? rauchen Sie?
   can I smoke? darf ich rauchen?
smooth glatt
   please try to smooth things over versuchen
   Sie bitte, die Angelegenheit in Ordnung zu
   bringen
   it all went very smoothly es ging alles ganz
   glatt
snack: can we just have a snack? können wir
   einen Imbiß bekommen?
» *TRAVEL TIP: you will find plenty of indoor and*
   outdoor snackbars called 'Schnellimbiß' or
   'Imbißstube' which sell sausages, chips etc
snow der Schnee
so so
   not so much nicht so viel
so so so la la
soap die Seife
sober nüchtern
social: this is a social visit ich bin privat *or*
   nicht geschäftlich hier
social security die Sozialversicherung
socks die Socken
soda (water) ein Soda(wasser)
Sofortreinigung (fast service) dry cleaner's
soft drink ein alkoholfreies Getränk
soft sell das Soft selling
software die Software
sole agency die Alleinvertretung
sole agent der Alleinvertreter
sole rights alleinige Rechte

....

Soll *debit*
solo: to go solo sich selbständig machen
solution die Lösung
some: some people einige Leute
    can I have some? kann ich etwas bekommen?
    can I have some leaflets? kann ich ein paar
    Prospekte bekommen?
    can I have some more? kann ich noch etwas
    bekommen?
    that's some drink! das ist vielleicht ein
    Getränk!
somebody jemand
something etwas
sometime irgendwann
sometimes manchmal
somewhere irgendwo
Sonderangebot *special offer*
soon bald
    as soon as possible so bald wie möglich
sooner eher
sore throat Halsschmerzen
sorry: (I'm sorry) Entschuldigung!
    we are sorry to hear ... es tut uns leid, daß ...
sort: this sort diese Art
    what sort of ...? was für ein ...?
    will you sort it out? können Sie das in
    Ordnung bringen?
south der Süden
South Africa Südafrika
South African südafrikanisch
South America Südamerika
souvenir ein Souvenir
space: extra space in the container
    zusätzlicher Raum im Container
    for reasons of space aus Platzgründen

ä [eh], au as in h*ow*, äu, eu [oy], ei as in I, ie [ee]
ö as in h*er*, ü, y as in h*u*ge, -b [-p], -d [-t], j [y], qu [kv]
s- [z-], ß [ss], v [f], w [v], z [ts]

Spain Spanien
Spanish spanisch
spare: spare part das Ersatzteil
speak: do you speak English? sprechen Sie
  Englisch?
  I don't speak ... ich kann kein ...
special besondere
  special terms besondere Bedingungen
  special case ein Sonderfall
specialist der Fachmann
specialize: we specialize in ... wir haben uns
  auf ... spezialisiert
specially besonders
specific speziell
specifications (*of equipment*) die technischen
  Daten
specify spezifizieren, genau angeben
  please specify time and place bitte geben
  Sie Zeit und Ort genau an
  please specify whether ... bitte geben Sie an,
  ob ...
  the items specified in our order die auf
  unserer Bestellung aufgeführten Artikel
  at the specified time/place zur angegebenen
  Zeit/am angegebenen Ort
specimen die Probe
spectacles die Brille
Spediteur carrier
speed die Geschwindigkeit
  speed is of the essence Schnelligkeit ist von
  ausschlaggebender Bedeutung
  please speed things up bitte beschleunigen
  Sie das
Speiseraum dining room
Speisewagen dining car
spell: how do you spell it? wie schreibt man
  das?
spend (*money*) ausgeben
Spesen expenses

spirits die Spirituosen
split (*costs etc*) aufteilen
spoon der Löffel
spot: our man on the spot unser Mann am Ort
sprain: I've sprained it ich habe es mir
  verstaucht
spring die Feder
  (*season*) der Frühling
square (*in town*) der Platz
  2 square metres zwei Quadratmeter
Staatsangehörigkeit nationality
staff das Personal
stage: at this stage of the work in diesem
  Stadium der Arbeit
staggered payments gestaffelte Zahlungen
stagnation die Stagnation
stairs die Treppe
stamp die Briefmarke
  two stamps for England zwei Briefmarken
  nach England
stand stehen
  (*at fair*) der Stand
  we stand by what we said wir bleiben bei
  dem, was wir gesagt haben
standard der Standard, die Norm
  British standards britische Normen
  (*adjective*) normal
stand-by (*ticket*) Standby
standing order ein Dauerauftrag
star der Stern
  a two/three/four/five-star hotel ein Zwei-/
  Drei-/Vier-/Fünf-Sterne-Hotel
start anfangen
  my car won't start mein Auto springt nicht
  an

ä [eh], au as in h*ow*, äu, eu [oy], ei as in I, ie [ee]
ö as in h*er*, ü, y as in h*u*ge, -b [-p], -d [-t], j [y], qu [kv]
s- [z-], ß [ss], v [f], w [v], z [ts]

....

when does it start? wann fängt es an?
starting next month ab nächsten Monat
starving: I'm starving ich habe einen
Riesenhunger
statement (*bank-*) der Auszug
(*from supplier etc*) die Rechnung
to make a statement on something eine
Erklärung über etwas abgeben
statement of account der Kontoauszug
station der Bahnhof
stay der Aufenthalt
we enjoyed our stay es hat uns gut gefallen
I'm staying at ... ich wohne in ...
steady (*increase, improvement*) ständig
steak ein Steak
YOU MAY HEAR ...
wie möchten Sie Ihr Steak gebraten haben?
ganz durch, halbdurch oder blutig?
*how would you like your steak done? well done,
medium or rare?*
steep: steep prices hohe Preise
steps: what steps are you taking? welche
Maßnahmen ergreifen Sie?
we'll take the necessary steps wir werden
die notwendigen Maßnahmen ergreifen
sterling Sterling
Steuer tax
Stichprobe spot check
sticking plaster ein (Heft)pflaster
still: we're still waiting for the goods wir
warten immer noch auf die Ware
they're still the best sie sind immer noch die
besten
stock der Bestand
stocks are running low die Lagerbestände
sind niedrig
they're out of stock sie sind nicht vorrätig
our current stock position unsere derzeitige
Bestandslage

we don't stock them any more die führen
wir nicht mehr
stock control die Bestandskontrolle
Stock Exchange die Börse
stockist der Händler
stock level die Lagerbestände
stock list die Warenliste
stomach der Magen
   I've got stomach-ache ich habe
   Magenschmerzen
   **have you got something for an upset
   stomach?** haben Sie etwas gegen
   Magenbeschwerden?
stone
» *1 stone=6.35 kilos*
stop: we intend to stop supplies unless ... wir
   beabsichtigen, die Lieferungen einzustellen, es
   sei denn ...
   please stop all work stellen Sie bitte die
   Arbeit ein
   do you stop near ...? halten Sie in der Nähe
   von ...?
   stop! halt!
stop-over die Zwischenstation
stoppage die Unterbrechung
store (*shop*) das Geschäft
storm der Sturm
stornieren to cancel
strafbar: ... ist strafbar ... is an offence
straight gerade
   go straight on gehen Sie geradeaus
   straight away sofort
   straight whisky Whisky pur
straight: let's get this straight das wollen wir
   mal klarstellen

ä [eh], au as in h*ow*, äu, eu [oy], ei as in I, ie [ee]
ö as in h*er*, ü, y as in h*u*ge, -b [-p], -d [-t], j [y], qu [kv]
   s- [z-], ß [ss], v [f], w [v], z [ts]

we've always been straight with you wir
sind immer offen und ehrlich zu Ihnen
gewesen
strange fremd
  (*odd*) seltsam
stranger der Fremde
  I'm a stranger here ich bin hier fremd
strategy die Strategie
streamlined rationalisiert
street die Straße
strength die Stärke
stress der Streß
  he's suffering from stress er leidet unter
  Streß
  I want to stress the importance of this ich
  möchte die Wichtigkeit dieser Angelegenheit
  betonen
strike der Streik
string: have you got any string? haben Sie
  Schnur?
stringent streng
strong stark
structure die Struktur
study: I want to study the figures ich möchte
  die Zahlen überprüfen
stupid dumm
style der Stil
**subcontract: if you subcontract the work
  to ...** wenn Sie die Arbeit vertraglich an ...
  weitergeben
subcontractor der Zulieferer
subject to vorbehaltlich
submit: to submit a report einen Bericht
  vorlegen
subscriber der Abonnent
subscription das Abonnement [abonnuh-mon]
  to take out a subscription to something
  etwas abonnieren
subsidiary die Tochtergesellschaft

succeed Erfolg haben
  if you succeed in improving sales wenn Sie
  den Absatz steigern können
success der Erfolg
  I wish you every success ich wünsche Ihnen
  viel Erfolg
successful erfolgreich
such: such a lot so viel
suddenly plötzlich
sue verklagen
  we intend to sue ... wir beabsichtigen, ... zu
  verklagen
  to sue for £50,000 auf £50.000 Schadenersatz
  verklagen
suffer: sales have suffered der Absatz hat
  gelitten
sugar der Zucker
suit (*man's*) der Anzug
  (*woman's*) das Kostüm
suitable passend
  not suitable for ... für ... nicht geeignet
suitcase der Koffer
summary eine Zusammenfassung
summer der Sommer
sun die Sonne
Sunday Sonntag
supermarket der Supermarkt
**supersede: the model has been superseded
  by ...** das Modell wurde von ... abgelöst
supper das Abendessen
supplier der Lieferant
  our suppliers unsere Lieferanten
supply (*customer*) beliefern
  (*goods*) liefern
  supply and demand Angebot und Nachfrage

ä [eh], au as in h*ow*, äu, eu [oy], ei as in I, ie [ee]
ö as in h*er*, ü, y as in h*u*ge, -b [-p], -d [-t], j [y], qu [kv]
s- [z-], ß [ss], v [f], w [v], z [ts]

continuity of supply die Kontinuität der
Lieferung
it's basically a supply problem das ist im
Prinzip eine Versorgungsfrage
our supplies are running out unsere Vorräte
gehen zur Neige
a new source of supply eine neue Quelle
can you supply us with ...? können Sie uns
mit ... beliefern?
we can supply them at 20% discount wir
können sie mit zwanzig Prozent Rabatt liefern
**the various services/products which we
can supply** die verschiedenen
Dienstleistungen/Produkte, die wir anbieten
können
support: we need your support wir brauchen
Ihre Unterstützung
sure: I'm not sure ich bin nicht sicher
are you sure? sind Sie sicher?
please make sure that ... bitte vergewissern
Sie sich, daß ...
I'm sure you will like the product ich bin
sicher, daß Ihnen das Produkt zusagt
surname der Nachname
survey (*of market*) die Marktforschung
(*of property*) ein Gutachten
suspend (*order*) einstellen
Sweden Schweden
Swedish schwedisch
Swiss Schweizer
(*person*) Schweizer/Schweizerin
switch der Schalter
to switch on/off anschalten/abschalten
Switzerland die Schweiz
in Switzerland in der Schweiz
symbol das Symbol
**sympathetic: we are very sympathetic with
your position** wir haben für Ihre Position
großes Verständnis

table ein Tisch
  a table for 4 ein Tisch für vier Personen
table wine Tafelwein
tailor: tailored to your requirements auf Ihre
  Bedürfnisse zugeschnitten
take nehmen
  can I take this with me? kann ich das
  mitnehmen?
  we'll take a thousand of each wir nehmen je
  tausend
  will you take them back? werden Sie sie
  zurücknehmen?
  to take out an insurance policy eine
  Versicherung abschließen
  will you take me to the airport? können Sie
  mich zum Flughafen bringen?
  the plane takes off at ... die Maschine geht
  um ...
  it will take 3 months es wird drei Monate
  dauern
  somebody has taken my bags jemand hat
  mein Gepäck mitgenommen
  I'll take you up on that ich nehme Sie beim
  Wort
takeover die Übernahme
takeover bid das Übernahmeangebot
talk sprechen
talks die Gespräche
tampons die Tampons
tape das Tonband
tape-recorder das Tonbandgerät
target das Ziel
  to set a target ein Ziel setzen
  we're on target es läuft nach Plan
  we're behind target wir sind im Verzug

ä [eh], au as in how, äu, eu [oy], ei as in I, ie [ee]
ö as in her, ü, y as in huge, -b [-p], -d [-t], j [y], qu [kv]
s- [z-], ß [ss], v [f], w [v], z [ts]

target date der Abschlußtermin
target market die Zielgruppe
tariff der Tarif
  (*in hotels*) die Preisliste
taste der Geschmack
  it tastes horrible/very nice das schmeckt
  fürchterlich/sehr gut
tax: **before tax** vor Abzug der Steuern, brutto
  after tax nach Abzug der Steuern, netto
taxi ein Taxi
  will you get me a taxi? rufen Sie mir bitte ein
  Taxi?
  where can I get a taxi? wo bekomme ich ein
  Taxi?
tax return die Steuererklärung
tea der Tee
  could I have a cup/pot of tea? könnte ich
  bitte eine Tasse/ein Kännchen Tee haben?
  YOU MAY THEN HEAR …
  mit Zitrone? *with lemon?*
  no, with milk, please nein, mit Milch, bitte
team das Team
teamwork Teamwork
technical technisch
  the technical departments die technischen
  Abteilungen
technician der Techniker
technology die Technologie
telegram ein Telegramm
  I want to send a telegram ich möchte ein
  Telegramm aufgeben
telephone das Telefon
  can I make a phone-call? kann ich bitte mal
  telefonieren?
  can I speak to …? kann ich bitte … sprechen?
  I'll telephone you when I get back ich rufe
  Sie an, wenn ich zurück bin
  as I mentioned on the telephone wie ich
  bereits am Telefon erwähnte

further to our recent telephone conversation bezugnehmend auf unser letztes Telefongespräch
telephone directory das Telefonbuch
» *TRAVEL TIP: lift receiver, money in, dial; unused coins returned; for international calls look for boxes with green disc with 'Ausland' or 'International'; code for UK from West Germany, Austria and Switzerland is 0044 and drop first 0 of UK area code; code from GDR is 06441*
YOU MAY HEAR ...
wen darf ich melden? *who's calling please?*
am Apparat *speaking*
Sie sind falsch verbunden *you've got the wrong number*
Augenblick bitte *one moment please*
kein Anschluß unter dieser Nummer *number no longer in use*
bitte warten *please wait*
television das Fernsehen
telex ein Fernschreiben, ein Telex
by telex per Telex
telex transfer der Telex-Transfer
tell: could you tell me where ...? könnten Sie mir bitte sagen, wo ...?
could you tell him that ... könnten Sie ihm bitte ausrichten, daß ...
as I told you at our last meeting wie ich Ihnen bei unserer letzten Besprechung sagte
as I told your colleague wie ich Ihrem Kollegen sagte
temperature die Temperatur
he has a temperature er hat Fieber
temporary vorübergehend

ä [eh], au as in h*ow*, äu, eu [oy], ei as in I, ie [ee]
ö as in h*er*, ü, y as in h*u*ge, -b [-p], -d [-t], j [y], qu [kv]
s- [z-], ß [ss], v [f], w [v], z [ts]

tender das Angebot
  we are interested in tendering for this contract wir möchten uns an dieser Ausschreibung beteiligen
Termin date; meeting; deadline
terminate (*agreement*) rückgängig machen
termination (*cancellation*) die Aufhebung (*expiry*) der Ablauf
terminus die Endstation
terms die Bedingungen
  what are your terms? wie sind Ihre Bedingungen?
  improved terms verbesserte Bedingungen
  under the terms of the agreement nach den Vereinbarungsbedingungen
terrible schrecklich
test der Test
  it's still being tested es wird immer noch getestet
than als
  bigger/better than ... größer/besser als ...
thanks, thank you danke(schön)
  thank you very much vielen Dank
  YOU MAY THEN HEAR ...
  bitteschön, bitte sehr *you're welcome*
  thank you for your letter vielen Dank für Ihr Schreiben
that dieser/diese/dieses
  I'd like that one ich möchte das da
  I think that ... ich glaube, daß ...
  that was ... das war ...
the der/die/das
  (*plural*) die
theatre das Theater
their ihr
  it's their idea/it's theirs das ist ihre Idee/das ist ihre
them sie
  with them mit ihnen

....

then (*at that time*) dann
  (*after that*) danach
  (*therefore*) deshalb
there dort
  how do I get there? wie komme ich dahin?
  is there/are there ...? gibt es ...?
  there you are (*giving*) bitte(schön)
these diese
they sie
  they are sie sind
thick dick
thin dünn
thing das Ding
  I've lost all my things ich habe alle meine
  Sachen verloren
think denken
  I'll think it over ich werde darüber
  nachdenken
  I think so/I don't think so ich glaube schon/
  ich glaube nicht
third dritte(r,s)
thirsty: I'm thirsty ich habe Durst
this dieser/diese/dieses
  can I have this one? kann ich das haben?
  this is Mr .../Mrs ... (das ist) Herr .../Frau ...
those diese (da)
  those people diese Leute (da)
through durch
Thursday Donnerstag
ticket (*train*) die Fahrkarte
  (*bus*) der Fahrschein
  (*plane*) das Ticket
  (*cinema*) die Eintrittskarte
  (*cloakroom*) die Garderobenmarke
» *TRAVEL TIP: see* **bus**

ä [eh], au as in h*ow*, äu, eu [oy], ei as in I, ie [ee]
ö as in h*er*, ü, y as in h*u*ge, -b [-p], -d [-t], j [y], qu [kv]
    s- [z-], ß [ss], v [f], w [v], z [ts]

tie (*necktie*) die Krawatte
  I'm tied up all day ich bin den ganzen Tag
  beschäftigt
  I want to get all the details tied up ich
  möchte alle Einzelheiten festlegen
Tiefgarage *underground parking*
tight (*schedule*) knapp bemessen
  (*control*) streng
  (*margin*) eng
  it's tight but I think we'll make it es ist
  knapp, aber ich glaube, wir schaffen es
tights die Strumpfhose
time die Zeit
  what's the time? wie spät ist es?
  I haven't got time ich habe keine Zeit
  for the time being vorläufig
  this time/last time/next time dieses Mal/
  letztes Mal/nächstes Mal
  3 times dreimal
  3 times as fast dreimal so schnell
  it takes a lot of time das dauert sehr lange
  to arrive in time rechtzeitig ankommen
  to arrive on time pünktlich ankommen
  it's a question of time das ist eine Frage der
  Zeit
  we need more time wir brauchen mehr Zeit
  we can't give you any more time wir können
  Ihnen nicht mehr Zeit geben
  have a good time! viel Spaß!
» *how to tell the time*
  it's one o'clock es ist ein Uhr
  it's 2/3/4/5/6 o'clock es ist zwei/drei/vier/fünf/
  sechs Uhr
  it's 5/10/20/25 past 7 es ist fünf/zehn/zwanzig/
  fünfundzwanzig (Minuten) nach sieben
  it's quarter past 8/8.15 es ist Viertel nach
  acht/acht Uhr fünfzehn
  it's half past 9/9.30 es ist halb zehn/neun Uhr
  dreißig

it's 25/20 to ten es ist fünf/zehn nach halb zehn
it's quarter to eleven es ist Viertel vor elf
it's 10/5 to eleven es ist zehn/fünf (Minuten)
vor elf
it's twelve o'clock es ist zwölf (Uhr)
at ... um ...
» *TRAVEL TIP: notice that in German half past
nine etc is said as 'half ten'!*
time-and-motion study eine Zeitstudie
time-consuming zeitaufwendig
time limit die Frist
timetable (*travel*) der Fahrplan
timing das Timing
  let's talk about the timing of the payments
  wir wollen die Zahlungstermine besprechen
  it's all a question of timing das ist eine Frage
  des Timing
  what's the timing on this? wie sieht's
  terminmäßig aus?
tip das Trinkgeld
  is the tip included? ist das inklusive
  Bedienung?
» *TRAVEL TIP: tip same people as in UK; also
customary to tip in pubs; tip not normally left
on the table*
tired müde
  I'm tired ich bin müde
tiring: it's tiring es ist anstrengend
tissues Papiertaschentücher
to: to England/Munich nach England/München
  to the factory zur Fabrik
  we'll send it to you wir schicken es Ihnen zu
today heute
  a week/a month today heute in einer Woche/
  einem Monat

ä [eh], au as in h*ow*, äu, eu [oy], ei as in I, ie [ee]
ö as in h*er*, ü, y as in h*u*ge, -b [-p], -d [-t], j [y], qu [kv]
s- [z-], ß [ss], v [f], w [v], z [ts]

together zusammen
  together with zusammen mit
  we're together wir sind zusammen (hier)
  can we pay all together? können wir alles
  zusammen bezahlen?
toilet die Toilette
  where are the toilets? wo sind die Toiletten?
» *TRAVEL TIP: see* **public conveniences**
tomato juice ein Tomatensaft
tomorrow morgen
  tomorrow morning morgen früh
  tomorrow afternoon morgen nachmittag
  tomorrow evening morgen abend
  the day after tomorrow übermorgen
  see you tomorrow bis morgen
  a week tomorrow morgen in einer Woche
ton die Tonne
» *1 ton=1,016 kilos*
tonic(water) ein Tonic(water)
tonight heute abend
tonne die Tonne
» *1 tonne=1000 kilos=metric ton*
too zu
  (*also*) auch
  that's too much das ist zuviel
tool das Werkzeug
  we are still tooling up wir sind immer noch
  beim Maschinenaufstellen
tooth der Zahn
  I've got toothache ich habe Zahnschmerzen
toothbrush eine Zahnbürste
toothpaste die Zahnpasta
top: on top of ... auf ...
  on the top floor im obersten Stock
  at the top oben
  top management das Spitzen-Management
  our top salesman unser Spitzenverkäufer
topic das Thema
top secret streng geheim

total die Endsumme
   that makes a total of ... das beträgt
   insgesamt ...
totally total
touch: we'll get in touch with you wir setzen
   uns mit Ihnen in Verbindung
   please get in touch with ... setzen Sie sich
   bitte mit ... in Verbindung
   please keep in touch bleiben Sie bitte mit
   uns in Verbindung
   **if you could put me in touch with someone
   who ...** wenn Sie mich mit jemand in
   Verbindung bringen könnten, der ...
tough (*competition etc*) hart
   (*material*) strapazierfähig
towards gegen
towel ein Handtuch
town die Stadt
   in town in der Stadt
   would you take me into town? könnten Sie
   mich bitte in die Stadt fahren?
trade der Handel
   people in the trade Leute vom Fach
trade fair die Messe
trader der Händler
trade secret ein Geschäftsgeheimnis
trade union die Gewerkschaft
trading deficit das Handelsdefizit
trading profit der Handelsgewinn
trading surplus der Handelsüberschuß
traditional traditionell
   the traditional approach die übliche
   Methode
   in the traditional way auf traditionelle Art
   und Weise

ä [eh], au as in h*o*w, äu, eu [oy], ei as in I, ie [ee]
ö as in h*er*, ü, y as in h*u*ge, -b [-p], -d [-t], j [y], qu [kv]
s- [z-], ß [ss], v [f], w [v], z [ts]

traffic lights die Ampel
train der Zug
» *TRAVEL TIP: efficient and punctual; if you travel Intercity buy your 'Zuschlag' (surcharge ticket) first*
YOU MAY HEAR ...
noch jemand zugestiegen? *any more tickets, please?*
trainee der Praktikant, der Auszubildende
training die Ausbildung
tranquillizers Beruhigungsmittel
transfer (*of money*) der Transfer, die Überweisung
  the sum has been transferred to your account der Betrag wurde auf Ihr Konto überwiesen
  he's been transferred to the Birmingham branch er wurde in die Zweigstelle nach Birmingham versetzt
transformer der Trafo
transit der Transit, die Durchfahrt (*of goods*) der Transport
  in transit auf der Durchreise
  damaged in transit auf dem Transport beschädigt
transit visa das Transitvisum
translate übersetzen
  would you translate that for me? könnten Sie das bitte für mich übersetzen?
translation die Übersetzung
translator der Übersetzer
transport der Transport
  has transport been arranged for us? ist das Transportproblem gelöst?
  transport charges die Transportkosten
transshipment die Umladung
travel reisen
travel agency das Reisebüro
traveller's cheque der Reisescheck

travelling salesman der Handelsreisende, der Vertreter
Treffen meeting
tremendous enorm
trend der Trend, die Tendenz
trial (*in court*) das Gerichtsverfahren
  on a trial basis auf Probe
  trials are still being carried out es werden immer noch Tests gemacht
trial order der Probeauftrag
trial period die Probezeit
trial run der Probelauf
trip: the trip out die Hinreise
  the trip back die Rückreise
trouble die Schwierigkeiten
  I'm having trouble with ... ich habe Schwierigkeiten mit ...
  that's just the trouble! genau das ist das Problem
  no trouble kein Problem
trouble-free problemlos
trouble-shooter (*mediator*) der Vermittler
trousers die Hose
true wahr
  it's not true das ist nicht wahr
trust: I trust you ich vertraue Ihnen
  we have to trust each other wir müssen einander vertrauen
  it's based on trust das beruht auf Vertrauen
trustee der Bevollmächtigte
trustworthy vertrauenswürdig
try versuchen
  we'll give it a try wir probieren es
  please try to convince him bitte versuchen Sie, ihn zu überzeugen

---

ä [eh], au as in h*ow*, äu, eu [oy], ei as in I, ie [ee]
ö as in h*er*, ü, y as in h*u*ge, -b [-p], -d [-t], j [y], qu [kv]
s- [z-], ß [ss], v [f], w [v], z [ts]

Tuesday Dienstag
turn: it's our turn to ... wir sind an der Reihe, ...
zu ...
  as it turned out wie sich herausgestellt hat
turnover der Umsatz
  an increase in turnover eine
  Umsatzsteigerung
turn(a)round die Bearbeitungszeit
  what sort of turn(a)round can you give us?
  mit welcher Bearbeitungszeit müssen wir
  rechnen?
  their turn(a)round time is much too slow
  sie haben eine viel zu lange Bearbeitungszeit
twice zweimal
  twice as much doppelt soviel
twin beds zwei (Einzel)betten
type: this type of ... diese Art von ...
  which type? welche Art?
  suitable for all types of ... für alle Arten von
  ... geeignet
  would you get this typed out for me?
  könnten Sie das bitte für mich tippen lassen?
typewriter eine Schreibmaschine
typical typisch
typist die Schreibkraft
U-Bahn underground
Übereinkunft agreement
Überstunden overtime
Übertrag amount brought forward
ulcer ein Magengeschwür
Ulster Ulster
umbrella der Schirm
Umleitung diversion
un- un-, nicht
unabhängig independent
unacceptable nicht akzeptabel, nicht
  annehmbar
under unter
  under 20% unter zwanzig Prozent

under the terms of the contract nach den
Vertragsbedingungen
undercapitalized unterkapitalisiert
undercut: we can undercut their prices wir
können ihre Preise unterbieten
underdone (*not cooked*) noch nicht gar
underestimate unterschätzen
underground (*rail*) die U-Bahn [oo-]
underpaid unterbezahlt
underpriced zu billig
understaffed unterbesetzt
understand: I understand ich verstehe
I don't understand das verstehe ich nicht
do you understand? verstehen Sie?
understanding: if we can reach an
understanding about the ... wenn wir eine
Vereinbarung über die ... treffen können
unexpected unerwartet
unfounded unbegründet
unfriendly unfreundlich
unhappy unglücklich
I'm still unhappy about it ich bin immer
noch nicht damit zufrieden
union (*trade-*) die Gewerkschaft
unit die Einheit
unit cost die Stückkosten
United States die Vereinigten Staaten
unit price der Stückpreis
Unkosten costs; expenses
unless: unless you can do it by next
Wednesday es sei denn, Sie können es bis
(spätestens) nächsten Mittwoch erledigen
unlikely unwahrscheinlich
Unternehmen firm, company; venture
Unterschrift signature

ä [eh], au as in h*ow*, äu, eu [oy], ei as in I, ie [ee]
ö as in h*er*, ü, y as in h*u*ge, -b [-p], -d [-t], j [y], qu [kv]
s- [z-], ß [ss], v [f], w [v], z [ts]

until bis
  until recently bis vor kurzem
  not until Tuesday nicht vor Dienstag
unusual ungewöhnlich
up: sales are up 10% der Verkauf ist um zehn
  Prozent gestiegen
  5% up on last year fünf Prozent höher als im
  Vorjahr
  when the extra period is up wenn die
  Verlängerung abgelaufen ist
  up to yesterday bis gestern
  up to 500 bis zu 500
  he's not up yet er ist noch nicht auf
up-market anspruchsvoll
up-to-date aktuell
  to keep the records up to date die
  Dokumentation auf dem laufenden halten
  **will you bring me up to date on what's
  happening?** würden Sie mich bitte über den
  neuesten Stand der Dinge informieren?
up-to-the-minute (*news, report*)
  allerneueste(r,s)
upturn ein Aufschwung
upwards: the trend is still upwards es besteht
  immer noch ein Aufwärtstrend
**urgency: please treat this as a matter of the
  greatest urgency** behandeln Sie das bitte als
  sehr dringend
urgent dringend
Urkunde document
us uns
  it's us das sind wir
use: can I use ...? kann ich ... benutzen?
useful nützlich
usual(ly) gewöhnlich
  as usual wie gewöhnlich
usw.=und so weiter etc
U-turn (*in policy*) eine Wende
vacancy (*job*) eine freie Stelle

valid gültig
  how long is it valid for? wie lange gilt es?
valuable wertvoll
value der Wert
  we value the work you've done wir wissen
  Ihre Arbeit zu schätzen
VAT die Mehrwertsteuer, MwSt (*not spoken*)
VEB = Volkseigener Betrieb (*in GDR*) *state-owned business*
vegetarian Vegetarier/Vegetarierin
verboten *forbidden*
Vereinbarung *agreement*
verify (*check*) (über)prüfen
Verkauf *sale*
Verkäufer *seller*
Vermögen *assets*
Verpackung *packing; packaging*
Versand *despatch*
verschiffen *to ship*
Verschleiß *wear and tear; (in Austria) retail trade*
Versicherung *insurance*
Verteilung *distribution*
Vertreter *agent, representative*
Vertretung *agency*
Vertretungsabkommen *agency agreement*
Vertrag *contract*
vertraglich *contractual*
Vertrieb *distribution*
very sehr
  very much better sehr viel besser
  I very much hope so das hoffe ich stark
vested interest persönliches Interesse
via über
view: in view of ... aufgrund ...

ä [eh], au as in h*ow*, äu, eu [oy], ei as in I, ie [ee]
ö as in h*er*, ü, y as in h*u*ge, -b [-p], -d [-t], j [y], qu [kv]
s- [z-], ß [ss], v [f], w [v], z [ts]

....

vintage der Jahrgang
visa ein Visum
visit der Besuch
  on our last visit to your factory bei unserem
  letzten Besuch Ihrer Fabrik
  we look forward to Herr Milbrandt's visit
  wir sehen dem Besuch von Herrn Milbrandt
  mit Interesse entgegen
vokda ein Wodka
voice die Stimme
voltage die Spannung
volume das Volumen
Vorbehalt proviso
Vorschrift regulation
Vorsicht! caution
Vorsicht Stufe mind the step
Vorstand board (of directors)
Vortrag carried forward
Währung currency
wait: will we have to wait long? werden wir
  lange warten müssen?
  don't wait for me warten Sie nicht auf mich
  I'm waiting for my colleague ich warte auf
  meinen Kollegen
waiter der Kellner
  waiter! Herr Ober!
waitress die Kellnerin
  waitress! Fräulein!
wake: will you wake me up at 7.30? würden
  Sie mich bitte um sieben Uhr dreißig wecken?
Wales Wales
walk: can we walk there? können wir da zu
  Fuß hingehen?
wall die Mauer
  (inside) die Wand
wallet die Brieftasche
want: I want a ... ich möchte ein ...
  I want to talk to ... ich möchte mit ... sprechen
  what do you want? was möchten Sie?

I don't want to ich will nicht
he wants to ... er will ...
they don't want to sie wollen nicht
he didn't want to er wollte nicht
warehouse das Lager
warehouse manager der Lagerverwalter
warehousing costs die Lagerkosten
Waren goods
Warenzeichen trademark
warm warm
warning die Warnung
warranty die Garantie
  it's under warranty darauf ist Garantie
Wartesaal waiting room
was: I was/he was/it was ich war/er war/es war
wash: can you wash these for me? könnten
  Sie das bitte für mich waschen?
watch (*wrist-*) die (Armband)uhr
  will you watch ...for me? würden Sie bitte für
  mich auf ... aufpassen?
  watch out! Achtung!
water das Wasser
  can I have some water? kann ich bitte etwas
  Wasser haben?
way: this is the way we see things developing
  wir stellen uns vor, daß sich die Dinge so
  entwickeln
  OK, let's do it your way okay, machen wir es
  auf Ihre Art
  the goods are on their way die Waren sind
  unterwegs
  could you tell me the way to ...? könnten Sie
  mir bitte sagen, wie ich zu/nach ... komme?
  see **where** *for answers*
waybill der Frachtbrief

ä [eh], au as in h*ow*, äu, eu [oy], ei as in I, ie [ee]
ö as in h*er*, ü, y as in h*u*ge, -b [-p], -d [-t], j [y], qu [kv]
  s- [z-], ß [ss], v [f], w [v], z [ts]

we wir
  we are wir sind
weak schwach
wear and tear der Verschleiß
weather das Wetter
  what filthy weather! so ein scheußliches
  Wetter!
Wechsel *bill of exchange; exchange*
Wechselkurs *rate of exchange*
Wednesday Mittwoch
week die Woche
  a week today/tomorrow heute/morgen in
  einer Woche
  in a week in einer Woche
  at the weekend am Wochenende
weigh wiegen
weight das Gewicht
weighting die Zulage
welcome: thank you for your warm welcome
  vielen Dank für Ihre freundliche Aufnahme
  welcome to ... willkommen in ...
  we would welcome your comments wir
  würden uns über Ihr Urteil freuen
well gut
  I'm not feeling well ich fühle mich nicht wohl
  he's not well es geht ihm nicht gut
  how are you? very well, thanks, and you?
  wie geht's? danke, ausgezeichnet, und Ihnen?
  you speak English very well Sie sprechen
  sehr gut Englisch
Welsh walisisch
Werbung *promotion; publicity*
were: you were Sie waren
  (familiar form) du warst
  you were *(plural)* Sie waren
  (familiar) ihr wart
  we were wir waren
  they were sie waren
Wert *value*

west der Westen
West Indies die westindischen Inseln
wet naß
what was
  what is that? was ist das?
  what for? wozu?
when? wann?
  when I arrived als ich ankam
  when I arrive wenn ich ankomme
where wo
  where is the post office? wo ist das Postamt?
  YOU MAY THEN HEAR ...
  geradeaus *straight on*
  erste Querstraße links/rechts *first left/right*
  an der Ampel vorbei *past the traffic lights*
whether ob
which welcher/welche/welches
  which one? welcher?
  YOU MAY THEN HEAR ...
  dieser/diese/dieses *this one*
  der da/die da/das da *that one*
  der/die/das linke *the one on the left*
whisky ein Whisky
white weiß
Whitsun Pfingsten
whizzkid ein Senkrechtstarter
who wer
wholesale der Großhandel
wholesale prices die Großhandelspreise
wholesaler der Großhändler
whose wessen
  whose is this? wem gehört das?
  YOU MAY THEN HEAR ...
  (das gehört) ihm/ihr/mir *(it belongs) to him/her/me*

ä [eh], au as in h*ow*, äu, eu [oy], ei as in I, ie [ee]
ö as in h*er*, ü, y as in h*u*ge, -b [-p], -d [-t], j [y], qu [kv]
s- [z-], ß [ss], v [f], w [v], z [ts]

....

why warum
  why not? warum nicht?
wide weit
wife: my wife meine Frau
will: we'll think about it wir werden es uns
  überlegen
  will he agree? wird er zustimmen?
  when will it be finished? wann ist es fertig?
  will you do it? tun Sie es?
willing: are you willing? sind Sie dazu bereit?
  we are willing to try it wir sind bereit, es
  auszuprobieren
win gewinnen
  (*order, contract*) bekommen
window das Fenster
  near the window am Fenster
wine der Wein
  can I see the wine list? kann ich die
  Getränkekarte haben?; *see pages 182–184*
winter der Winter
wire der Draht; (*elec*) die Leitung
wise (*policy, decision*) vernünftig
  I think it would be wise to ... ich glaube, es
  wäre vernünftig, ... zu ...
wish: best wishes alles Gute
  please give my best wishes to Herr Polde
  bitte richten Sie Herrn Polde freundliche
  Grüße aus
  Mr Gordon sends his best wishes Herr
  Gordon läßt freundliche Grüße ausrichten
  the customers' wishes die Wünsche der
  Kunden
with mit
withdraw (*money from account*) abheben
  if we withdraw from the project falls wir
  uns von dem Projekt zurückziehen
within: within 3 months innerhalb von drei
  Monaten
without ohne

witness der Zeuge
  will you act as a witness for me? würden Sie
  mein Zeuge sein?
woman die Frau
wonderful herrlich
wood das Holz
wool die Wolle
word das Wort
  I don't know that word das Wort kenne ich
  nicht
word processor eine Textverarbeitungs-
  maschine
work die Arbeit
  there's still a lot of work to do es gibt noch
  viel zu tun
  it's very complicated work das ist eine sehr
  komplizierte Arbeit
  (*verb*) arbeiten
  it's not working (*machine, plan*) es
  funktioniert nicht
  I work in London ich arbeite in London
  a good working relationship ein gutes
  Arbeitsverhältnis
  if we can work something out falls wir
  etwas ausarbeiten können
  it'll work out in the end das kriegen wir
  schon hin
workflow der Arbeitsablauf
workforce die Belegschaft
working capital das Betriebskapital
workload die Arbeit(belastung)
works der Betrieb, die Fabrik
world die Welt
  in the world auf der Welt
worldwide (*distribution, sales*) weltweit

ä [eh], au as in h*ow*, äu, eu [oy], ei as in I, ie [ee]
ö as in h*er*, ü, y as in h*u*ge, -b [-p], -d [-t], j [y], qu [kv]
s- [z-], ß [ss], v [f], w [v], z [ts]

Wine Guide

There is a huge variety of German wines and the vast majority of them (some 85%) are white. In general German wine is light and refreshing, a very versatile wine that can be drunk on any occasion. Strict government controls apply to production and this is reflected on the wine label. An ability to decipher the label is, therefore, useful as a guide to the contents of the bottle. The wine label will contain three main items:

1. the quality of the wine;
2. the wine-growing area from which the wine comes;
3. the type of grape.

All three of these items must be present on a bona fide German wine.

1. There are three quality gradings for German wine:

Tafelwein;
Qualitätswein;
Qualitätswein mit Prädikat.

Tafelwein (table wine) is the lightest grade of wine.
Qualitätswein has more body and must originate from one of the eleven approved wine-growing areas. A Qualitätswein will also have a government control number on the label.
Qualitätswein mit Prädikat is the top quality German wine. When this category is designated the sort of grape from which the wine is produced will also be given. These sorts of grape are:

Auslese (=selection) wine from the ripest bunches of grapes;
Beerenauslese wine from specially selected single grapes;

Eiswein a rare wine made from grapes picked
after the first touch of frost;
Kabinett the lightest wine in this category,
usually dry;
Sekt sparkling wine;
Spätlese (=late harvest) more body, rather
sweet;
Trockenbeerenauslese made from individually
selected dried grapes, a superb and very rare and
heady wine.

2. The eleven official wine-growing areas are (in
alphabetical order):

Ahr try this for red wines;
Baden strong aromatic wines;
Bergstraße very mellow, only whites;
Franken dry, sold in flagons (Bocksbeutel);
Mittelrhein light white wines;
Mosel-Saar-Ruwer sweet and delicate wines
mainly from Riesling grapes;
Nahe mainly Riesling grapes;
Rheingau try these elegant Rieslings
Rheinhessen aromatic, mainly Silvaner grapes;
Rheinpfalz full-bodied wines;
Württemberg very dry white wines; try this also
for red wines, especially a Trollinger.

3. The official types of grape used for German
wines are:

blauer Portugieser
Gewürztraminer
Kerner
Morio-Muskat
Müller-Thurgau

ä [eh], au as in h*ow*, äu, eu [oy], ei as in I, ie [ee]
ö as in h*er*, ü, y as in h*u*ge, -b [-p], -d [-t], j [y], qu [kv]
s- [z-], ß [ss], v [f], w [v], z [ts]

....

Riesling
Ruländer
Scheurebe
Silvaner
Spätburgunder (blauer)

In addition to the three basic quality gradings there is a further type of wine called 'deutscher Landwein', an inexpensive and very pleasant wine which is very popular with the Germans.

Some basic wine terms:

Weißwein *white wine*
Rotwein *red wine*
trocken *dry*
halbtrocken *semi-dry*
lieblich *mellow*
süß *sweet*
herb *very dry*

If you'd like something a little lighter try a 'Schorle'. 'Eine saure Schorle' is white wine and mineral water mixed half and half; 'eine süße Schorle' is white wine and lemonade mixed half and half. These are also called 'einen sauer-gespritzten Wein' and 'einen süß-gespritzten Wein'.
If you order a glass of wine this will normally be ¼ litre (ein Viertel); for a smaller glass ask for 'ein Achtel' (⅛ litre).

some useful phrases:
what would you recommend with ...? *was würden Sie zu ... empfehlen?*
I'd like something very dry/fairly sweet *ich hätte gern einen sehr trockenen Wein/einen ziemlich süßen Wein*
could we have another bottle please? *könnten wir bitte noch eine Flasche hiervon bekommen?*
cheers *Prost, zum Wohl* .

worry die Sorge
   I'm worried about it ich mache mir Sorgen
   darüber
   don't worry keine Sorge
worse: it's worse es ist schlimmer
   it's getting worse es wird schlimmer
worst schlechteste(r,s)
worth: it's not worth that much so viel ist das
   nicht wert
   is it worthwhile going to ...? lohnt es sich,
   nach ... zu gehen?
   it's not worth it das lohnt sich nicht
worthless wertlos
would: would you ...? würden Sie ...?
wrap: could you wrap it up? könnten Sie es
   bitte einpacken?
   to wrap up a deal ein Geschäft abschließen
wrapping die Verpackung
write schreiben
   could you write it down? könnten Sie das
   bitte aufschreiben?
   we'll be writing to you wir werden Ihnen
   schreiben
   could we have that in writing? könnten wir
   das bitte schriftlich haben?
   to write off losses Verluste abschreiben
writing paper das Schreibpapier
wrong falsch
   I think the invoice is wrong ich glaube, die
   Rechnung stimmt nicht
   there's something wrong with ... da stimmt
   etwas nicht mit ...
   you're wrong Sie irren sich
   sorry, wrong number tut mir leid, ich habe
   mich verwählt

ä [eh], au as in how, äu, eu [oy], ei as in I, ie [ee]
ö as in her, ü, y as in huge, -b [-p], -d [-t], j [y], qu [kv]
s- [z-], ß [ss], v [f], w [v], z [ts]

yard das Yard
» *1 yard=91.44 cms=0.91 m*
year das Jahr
yearly jährlich
yellow gelb
yellow pages das Branchenverzeichnis, die
  gelben Seiten
yes ja
  **you won't be able to manage that — oh yes,
  we can!** Sie werden das nicht schaffen — oh
  doch!
yesterday gestern
  the day before yesterday vorgestern
  yesterday morning/afternoon/evening
  gestern morgen/nachmittag/abend
yet: is it ready yet? ist es schon fertig?
  not yet noch nicht
you Sie
  (*familiar form*) du
  (*familiar plural*) ihr
  for you für Sie/dich/euch
  with you mit Ihnen/dir/euch
» *TRAVEL TIP: use the 'Sie' forms in most
  situations; the familiar 'du' forms are for people
  you know well; it's best to let the German
  speaker start using the 'du' form; examples are:
  Sie gehen/du gehst; Sie bleiben/du bleibst; in
  letters instead of 'du, dich, dir' etc write 'Du,
  Dich, Dir' etc; see also* **Christian name**
young jung
your Ihr
  (*familiar*) dein
  (*plural*) euer
  is this yours? gehört das Ihnen/dir?
Yugoslavia Jugoslawien
Yugoslavian jugoslawisch
Zahlung payment
z.B.=zum Beispiel e.g.
z.Hd.=zu Händen attn.

zero Null
   below zero unter Null
zero-rated ohne Mehrwertsteuer
ziehen pull
Zimmer frei vacancies, rooms
Zins interest
Zinssatz rate of interest
zip der Reißverschluß
Zoll Customs
Zollabfertigung Customs clearance
Zollager bonded warehouse
Zollerklärung Customs declaration
zollpflichtig dutiable
Zutritt verboten no admission
zu verkaufen for sale
zu vermieten for hire; to let
Zweigstelle branch
Zwischenhändler middleman

0	null	**1st**	erste, 1.
1	eins	**2nd**	zweite, 2.
2	zwei (*also* zwo)	**3rd**	dritte, 3.
3	drei	**4th**	vierte, 4.
4	vier	**5th**	fünfte, 5.
5	fünf	**6th**	sechste, 6.
6	sechs	**7th**	siebte, 7.
7	sieben	**8th**	achte, 8.
8	acht	**9th**	neunte, 9.
9	neun	**10th**	zehnte, 10.
10	zehn	**11th**	elfte, 11.
11	elf	**12th**	zwölfte, 12.
12	zwölf	**13th**	dreizehnte, 13.
13	dreizehn		etc
14	vierzehn	**20th**	zwanzigste, 20.
15	fünfzehn		etc
16	sechzehn		
17	siebzehn		
18	achtzehn		
19	neunzehn		
20	zwanzig		
21	einundzwanzig		
22	zweiundzwanzig		
23	dreiundzwanzig		
24	vierundzwanzig		
25	fünfundzwanzig		
26	sechsundzwanzig		
27	siebenundzwanzig		
28	achtundzwanzig		
29	neunundzwanzig		
30	dreißig		
40	vierzig		
50	fünfzig		
60	sechzig		
70	siebzig		
80	achtzig		
90	neunzig		
100	hundert		
101	hunderteins		

175 hundertfünfundsiebzig
200 zweihundert
1,000 tausend, 1.000, 1 000
2,000 zweitausend, 2.000, 2 000
2,469 zweitausendvierhundertneunundsechzig
1,000,000 eine Million, 1.000.000, 1 000 000
1,000,000,000 eine Milliarde, 1.000.000.000,
1 000 000 000

$\frac{1}{4}$ ein Viertel
$\frac{1}{3}$ ein Drittel
$\frac{1}{2}$ ein halb
$\frac{2}{3}$ zwei Drittel
$\frac{3}{4}$ Dreiviertel
$1\frac{1}{4}$ eineinviertel
$1\frac{1}{2}$ eineinhalb, anderthalb
$2\frac{1}{2}$ zweieinhalb
$\frac{1}{8}$ **etc** ein Achtel etc
0.2 null Komma zwei, 0,2
3.86 drei Komma sechsundachtzig, 3,86

Note that in German the comma is used as a decimal point and the full-stop is used for thousands.

4+4 vier plus vier
4−2 vier minus zwei
4×4 vier mal vier
4−2 vier geteilt durch zwei
4+4=8 vier plus vier gleich acht

40% of 35 vierzig Prozent von fünfunddreißig
30% increase eine Zunahme von 30%, eine
30%ige (dreißigprozentige) Zunahme

2² zwei quadrat
2³ zwei hoch 3
2⁴ zwei hoch 4

./. (in reports, accounts etc)=less

Special Vocabulary List

English/Englisch	German/Deutsch

Special Vocabulary List

English/Englisch	German/Deutsch

Special Vocabulary List

English/Englisch	German/Deutsch